SHIPWRECKS
of the
PACIFIC
NORTHWEST

SHIPWRECKS
of the
PACIFIC
NORTHWEST

TRAGEDIES AND LEGACIES
OF A PERILOUS COAST

EDITED BY JENNIFER KOZIK
MARITIME ARCHAEOLOGICAL SOCIETY

Globe
Pequot

Guilford, Connecticut

Globe
Pequot

An imprint of The Rowman & Littlefield Publishing Group, Inc.
4501 Forbes Blvd., Ste. 200
Lanham, MD 20706
www.rowman.com

Distributed by NATIONAL BOOK NETWORK

British Library Cataloguing in Publication Information available

Library of Congress Cataloging-in-Publication Data available

ISBN 978-1-4930-4453-5 (hardcover)
ISBN 978-1-4930-4454-2 (e-book)

♾™ The paper used in this publication meets the minimum requirements of American National Standard for Information Sciences—Permanence of Paper for Printed Library Materials, ANSI/NISO Z39.48-1992.

There is, one knows not what sweet mystery about this sea, whose gently awful stirrings seem to speak of some hidden soul beneath.

— Herman Melville

CONTENTS

FOREWORD

A striking curved roof, evocative of steep ocean waves, marks the Columbia River Maritime Museum. My office at the museum is within sight of the infamous Columbia River Bar, which has laid waste to countless sailors, boats, and ships from the time the earliest indigenous peoples paddled the Big River, or *Wimahl* in the Chinookan language, in their canoes until the present day.

Inside, a great wall map labeled "Graveyard of the Pacific" depicts the area around the mouth of the Columbia River. Stylized boat symbols mark the locations of fifty shipwrecks, only a fraction of the true number but enough to overwhelm visitors, who are frequently seen staring in wonder at the immensity of the loss that has occurred so close to where they stand.

The ability to devise methods of traveling across waters to other lands proved irresistible to ancient peoples across the globe. Various types of boats, beginning with rafts and dugout canoes, appear in both the archaeological and earliest written records of many civilizations. For millennia, men have taken to the sea, and for millennia, there they have died, their boats swamped and capsized or battered and torn by waves on rocks or sand.

The resulting shipwrecks have captured the imagination of storytellers and listeners, and readers, from the beginning; the fascination is well documented in literature throughout recorded history. See A. E. Stallings's excellent essay "Shipwreck Is Everywhere" (*Hudson Review*, Autumn 2017). The enduring appeal of a well-told tale of terror and loss on the high seas explains the surprising success of Canadian singer/songwriter Gordon Lightfoot's "Wreck of the Edmund Fitzgerald": "Does any one know where the love of God goes, when the waves turn the minutes to hours?"

Shipwrecks fascinate by combining a number of subjects that individually have long fascinated us, as reflected in literature and art: the sea, ships, sailing, exploration, adventure, storms, terror, and loss. When extensive documentation exists, in the form of the accounts of survivors, rescuers, and other eyewitnesses, we are enthralled by the true stories. In the absence of witnesses, our imaginations are set free to create the howling wind, the sound of the breakers growing louder, the terror of feeling the ship break apart under one's feet, the despairing realization that no help is coming, and the final capitulation to the tumbling, cold salt water.

If we are fortunate, historians, researchers, and archaeologists are able to find and study physical remains, as well as a written historical record, and slowly piece together a credible understanding of the ship, its crew, and the events that led to the wreck and aftermath. The physical study of the wreck adds to our knowledge of ship design and construction and other aspects of the scholarly record. For the general public, the human element is often more intriguing, and the focus of storytelling. When the technical and human aspects come together, a compelling story results.

With this new, well-told volume, the Maritime Archaeological Society (MAS) brings us nine such compelling stories. I applaud MAS's authors for their excellent work in bringing these very distinct shipwrecks so vividly to life, and nurturing our hunger for learning about our past.

One might presume that modern technology has made shipwrecks a rarity; on the contrary, in 2017 alone ninety-four large ships, and countless smaller vessels, were lost at sea worldwide. After a thirty-year career as a U.S. Coast Guard helicopter pilot, searching desolate debris fields for survivors, usually fruitlessly, and rescuing thankful survivors from boats in their death throes, I can testify to these truths: The sea remains unforgiving in its violence; ships remain breakable objects when subject to the sea's fury and careless treatment by their crews; and even the most experienced sailors remain fallible in their judgment. I have no doubt that a hundred years from now, a revised edition of *Shipwrecks of the Pacific Northwest* will recount new tragedies in the Graveyard of the Pacific on vessels not yet built today.

Captain Bruce Jones, U.S. Coast Guard (Retired)
Former Commander, Coast Guard Sector Columbia
River Deputy Director, Columbia River Maritime
Museum, Astoria, Oregon

PREFACE

It is difficult to decide when it is time to take all of the knowledge you have been collecting and turn it into a book. The Maritime Archaeological Society was a relatively new organization in June of 2018 when it was approached about providing a new look at local shipwrecks. Our core board members and researchers are all avid consumers of history. We are often frustrated with the way most of the books upheld as the definitive authorities on Northwest shipwrecks list no sources for their own research. Additionally, most of the books were written before archives and newspapers throughout the world began digitizing their collections and before Google began its initiative to make tens of millions of books and magazines available online. There are a couple of books on the Graveyard of the Pacific from the twenty-first century, but they tend to finish the same way. The stories end with the immediate aftermath of the shipwreck. As archaeologists, we want to know more about what happens to the tangible remains. Since we were seeking out these wrecks as part of our mission anyway, we decided to cannonball into the deep and write up what we hope is a helpful addition to the body of research on shipwrecks of Oregon and Washington. MAS is indebted to all of the primary researchers and contributing writers who helped make this book a reality: Scott Williams, Jeff Smith, Christopher Dewey, Tod Lundy, Jim Sharpe, Jeff Groth, and Robert Johnson.

INTRODUCTION

The Pacific Northwest has no shortage of shipwrecks. The stormy, rocky coastline and perilous river bars are often referred to as the Graveyard of the Pacific. The area stretches from Tillamook Bay on the northern coast of Oregon to the top of Vancouver Island in British Columbia. Thousands of ships have met their end here, and many of those ships have dramatic tales of heroism, death, and survival. Some books about shipwrecks in the region are thorough surveys of available archival materials, while others speculate about fantastical ship battles and buried pirate treasure. But where did those wrecks really end up? What is left of them today?

Standing on the beach, it is nearly impossible to believe a shipwreck might be directly underfoot. The hard, compact sand feels solid and permanent. To the human eye, it appears low and even, far up and down the beach. Then one night, when no one is watching, the surging tide of a big winter storm scrapes away that sand, revealing one hundred feet of wooden ribs from an old ship. A row of evenly spaced frames still point inward where the ship came to rest nearly perpendicular to the shoreline over a hundred years ago. It is easy now to imagine a ship plowing toward the beach from the sea on a long-ago dark, foggy night. Standing over the remains of the shipwreck is like looking at a skeleton in an opened tomb, revealing the long-hidden bones after whatever tragedy took away that life. The bones of the ship are saying they have more story left to tell.

Physical evidence of shipwrecks on beaches, underwater, and in museums provide a corporeal link to history. The Maritime Archae-ological Society (MAS) investigates and documents this physical evidence, sharing findings with the public and the state. When the interest of the public and the press is generated, the attention can help sway state historic preservation agencies to consider maritime sites a cultural resource worthy of protection. The group, MAS, was formed after seeing a need for a coordinated group of professional archaeologists and volunteers to document as well as advocate for shipwrecks and other submerged archaeological sites in the region. According to Dr. Dennis Griffin, archaeologist with the Oregon State Historic Preservation Office, there are over 3,000 shipwrecks off the coast of Oregon alone, while the number of reported shipwreck sites is just over 300. The list of sites verified by archaeologists is even smaller, numbering only around 140.[1]

A shipwreck goes through a lifecycle, beginning with the circumstances leading up to the wreck and ending when there are no physical remains left. Keith Muckelroy laid out the basics of what is called a shipwreck "site formation process" in his definitive 1978 book, *Maritime Archaeology*. It begins with the pre-impact conditions. For example, there may have been a big storm or mechanical problems that contributed to the disaster. Next, it is important to know about the impact of the crash and rescue of the persons on board. Learning details of the wreck from firsthand witness accounts helps explain what really happened to the ship. The ship may have, for instance, broken into multiple pieces as she went down. Whether or not there were salvage operations is important too. A wrecked ship may have been refloated, leaving nothing on the impact site to find. Metal hull plating may have been removed and sold. A wooden shipwreck may have been burned to expose valuable metal. It is important to know what may be left to document.

With the passage of time, a wreck left in place becomes an archaeological site. Perishables on the wreck site disintegrate and the seabed moves around. The shifting sands may routinely uncover and rebury parts of the ship. Perhaps a maritime archaeology team might one day circle around what remains, observing the distribution of materials and taking measurements.

Many shipwrecks are concentrated where the Columbia River narrows to a powerful funnel and meets the Pacific Ocean. At three miles wide and six miles long, the mouth of the river is considered one of the most dangerous stretches of water in the world. The area has shallow shoals and narrow sand deposits called spits everywhere, sometimes lurking just under the water. The Oregon State Marine Board details some of these perils. Just south of the Columbia River is Clatsop Spit. A state-issued guide to boating the Columbia River Bar states that "during flood currents and slacks, it may be relatively calm, with only a gentle swell breaking far in on the spit. Yet 5 or 10 minutes later, when the current has started to ebb, it can become extremely treacherous, with breakers extending far out toward the channel." On the north side is Peacock Spit, where the waves "break from three different directions. If you lose power on the bar during an ebb current, your vessel will be carried into Peacock Spit."

Columbia River Bar pilots have helped guide big ships in and out of the river since at least the early 1800s, when Chinook Chief Concomly regularly met incoming Hudson's Bay Company ships. His large cedar dugout canoe, with twenty paddlers, was efficient at navigating the treacherous waters of the *Wimahl*, or Big River. Concomly was a legendary figure in the area. Depictions of the chief show him with one eye and sometimes wearing a British red coat.

The Pacific Northwest waters generally have two high tides and two low tides each day. Water moves downstream away from shore during an ebb current, and upstream toward shore during a flood current. Ebb currents can be very strong, especially when runoff is feeding into the river. The US Coast Guard recommends crossing the bar during two key times. It is safest to cross during a slack tide, or during a flood tide, when conditions are usually the calmest. The river bar, or river entrance, is where the outgoing ebb current interacts with the ocean currents and sea swells.

Weather can be brutal in the region, especially when it comes to winter storms during the rainy season. The Pacific coast is a lee shore, meaning the waves, winds, and currents all invariably push unwary vessels toward the land, sometimes with disastrous results. Many Pacific Northwest shipwreck stories start out with sailors setting out in fair conditions and suddenly finding themselves trapped in a wild squall. Swells can come out of nowhere to toss ships around, and strong winds can blow them off course.

Winter storms can be helpful too. Strong tides sometimes uncover long-forgotten shipwrecks and artifacts, as was the case with two carronades from the wreck of the 1846 navy schooner USS *Shark* found on a beach in 2008. Changing conditions under the water can also alter what we think we know about a wreck. Additional wreckage uncovered at the National Register of Historic Places–listed site of the 1830 Hudson's Bay Company shipwreck *Isabella* has provided evidence that it might be an entirely different ship instead.

Remains of a ship, once uncovered, begin to go through changes. Underwater or in the tide line, waves can move everything around. On land, it might be exposure to the elements or curious humans that alter a wreck. For those of us on land who seek out shipwrecks, winter storms can completely uncover a long-forgotten shipwreck on the beach one day and then move, destroy, or bury the remains the next day, leaving no trace. Shipwreck documentarians often have to run out to investigate a site quickly before it is gone. When trying to tell the story of a wreck, it is a dynamic graveyard, a race against time and the elements.

Nearly everyone loves being near the ocean. Its vastness both isolates us and connects us to other places. The varying hues of blue are mesmerizing, while the smell of the salt air and the sound of the waves can have calming effects. The Pacific Northwest coastline, with its rugged shoreline trimmed by Douglas fir and cedar trees, is windy, foggy, and damp. But for some of us, there is no place we would rather be standing on this earth.

The deep, unknowable darkness of the water at night and the unrelenting swells of the waves are experiences only those who have spent time at sea can fully understand. Understanding how the sea makes us feel is material that has been explored by poets for ages: Kipling, Tennyson, Neruda. The experience of living through a shipwreck is something most of us can scarcely imagine. Ovid is quoted as saying, "The man who has experienced shipwreck shudders even at a calm sea."

It would take several more books and lifetimes of research to cover the maritime history of the entire Graveyard of the Pacific. *This book* will focus on the southern portion of the graveyard from Rockaway

Beach, just north of Tillamook Bay in Oregon, up to North Cove near Willapa Bay in Washington. It will cover the span of time from a Spanish galleon, *Santo Cristo de Burgos*, which wrecked before the last big Northwest mega-earthquake and tsunami in 1700, to a cargo ship named *Mauna Ala*, bound for Pearl Harbor just before the onset of American involvement in World War II.

Nonfiction does not need to be dry and colorless. Maritime history becomes palpable when its vivid stories are brought to life. The tales of people who lived and died at the mercy of the seas can be understood through their ships, their words, and by the events that shaped their lives. What follows are stories of heroism, bad luck, and all of the dramatic perils the sea has to offer. We will add to those stories by examining what tangible legacies remain today and what might still be out there, waiting to be found.

Jennifer Kozik

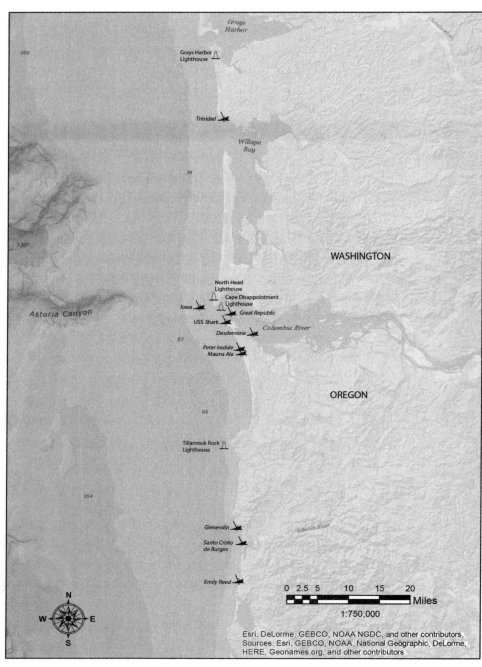

Grays
Harbor

Chehalis River

Grays Harbor
Lighthouse

160

Trinidad

Willapa
Bay

34

WASHINGTON

130?

North Head
Lighthouse

Cape Disappointment
Lighthouse

Astoria Canyon

Iowa

Great Republic

USS Shark

Columbia River

Desdemona

57

Peter Iredale
Mauna Ala

OREGON

65

Tillamook Rock
Lighthouse

164

Nehalem River

Glenesslin

Santo Cristo
de Burgos

Emily Reed

N
W   E
S

0   2.5 5   10   15   20
                                    Miles
1:750,000

Esri, DeLorme, GEBCO, NOAA NGDC, and other contributors,
Sources: Esri, GEBCO, NOAA, National Geographic, DeLorme,
HERE, Geonames.org, and other contributors

Courtesy of the Maritime Archaeological Society. Cartography by Jeff Groth

SANTO CRISTO DE BURGOS

SPANISH GALLEON AND BEESWAX WRECK MYSTERY AT NEHALEM, 1693–94

The Pacific Northwest was one of the last places in North America to be explored and settled by Europeans and Americans. Occasional brief visits of exploration and trade were made to the region during the later years of the eighteenth century, but the first permanent white settlement in the area was not until 1811. In that year, the fur-trading post of Astoria was founded near the mouth of the Columbia River. The fur traders endured a relatively isolated existence, relying on the goodwill of their Native American neighbors to bring furs and other goods to trade. Furs from the Pacific Northwest were shipped primarily to China. Known as "soft gold," the fur trade was a lucrative business while it lasted. Animals hunted for their fur, such as the beaver and otter, were nearly driven to extinction in the nineteenth century.

Among the items brought to trade at Fort Astoria by the Clatsop and Nehalem Indians were large, molded cakes of beeswax stamped with unusual symbols, numbers, and Latin letters. Knowing beeswax was not a locally available item, the traders asked the Nehalem and Clatsop about the source of the beeswax blocks and candles. The Indians said a large

1565 illustration of a galleon.

ship had wrecked on the beach at the Nehalem River many years prior to the arrival of the fur traders. The Nehalem River, about forty miles south of Astoria, is separated from the Pacific Ocean by a long, narrow sand spit. Prior to the introduction of nonnative beach grass and other plant species, the spit consisted of a series of low sand dunes that migrated across the spit with the prevailing winds, alternately exposing and burying the beeswax blocks, candles, and wrecked timbers of the ship.

A molded block of beeswax, stamped with a symbol, found at Nehalem Spit. **Courtesy of the Clatsop County Historical Society, Astoria. Photographer Jennifer Kozik**

In the middle of the twentieth century, Oregon State Parks began planting nonnative beach grass to make the spit more attractive for camping and recreation. With the beach grass trapping sand and preventing its movement, the dune on the seaward face of the spit rose from twenty to twenty-five feet in height to over forty-five feet high today. The dunes behind the seaward dune, on the river and bay side of the spit, are also locked in place by a mix of the beach grass, shore pines, and inadvertently introduced Scotch broom. There is no longer any wreckage or beeswax to be seen on the beach or spit, although pieces are occasionally found during construction in Nehalem Bay State Park or the nearby town of Manzanita.

The fur trader accounts are the first written record of what became an enduring Oregon mystery. Questions grew as to when the ship wrecked at Nehalem, where she had come from, where she was going, and most curious of all, why the ship had been carrying so much beeswax in the form of large candles and strangely marked cakes. The beeswax blocks and candles were scattered for miles over the spit and shores of the Nehalem River, including up into the lower Nehalem Valley. The majority of this material was found at elevations above the highest tide line, and often quite a distance inland from the ocean and river. Beeswax was also found on beaches to the north and south of Nehalem, but in much lower quantities and always in areas reached by ocean waves.

So much beeswax was scattered over Nehalem Spit and the lower valley that collecting beeswax to sell became a source of income for early settlers in the area, and its occurrence was remarked upon by nearly every visitor to the coast. The Beeswax Wreck, as it was called, and her cargo were the topics of much speculation in the scientific and popular press throughout the late nineteenth and early twentieth centuries. The amount of beeswax was so large that many observers were convinced that the wax must be a natural deposit of mineral wax rather than the cargo of a ship.[1]

To the early fur traders and later American settlers of the nineteenth century, and even into the twentieth century, the presence of a so-called ancient wreck on the shore of the Nehalem Spit was a continuing

Nehalem Spit in 1939, prior to introduced vegetation that locked the sand dunes in place.
Courtesy of Mark Beach

source of intrigue. The wreck was "ancient" in that she had obviously been there decades or even centuries prior to settlement of the coast by European and American immigrants. Questions about the origin of the mystery vessel and her cargo, as well as the fate of the crew, were debated in the press and scientific journals for decades.[2]

Over the years, as the beeswax blocks became harder to find and the wrecked timbers of the ship disappeared under the shifting sands or into the woodpiles of the local residents, interest in the story of the Beeswax Wreck waned. It was not until the final decades of the twentieth century that archaeologists began to address some of the questions surrounding the wreck. However, those initial investigations were limited in both scope and funding, and the archaeologists soon moved on to other projects.

In 2006 a volunteer group of professional archaeologists, historians, geologists, and interested community members began a coordinated effort to investigate the Beeswax Wreck in cooperation with the Oregon Parks and Recreation Department and Oregon State Historic Preservation Office. The goals of the project included determining the origin and nationality of the ship, locating wreck remains, and confirming the identity of the vessel. This group, known initially as the Beeswax Wreck Research Project and later as a project of the Maritime Archaeological Society, has conducted a variety of terrestrial and marine archaeological surveys, carried out intensive archival research, and offered public outreach in the form of community lectures, school talks, and tours. Based on the findings of the project, it is now known that the Beeswax Wreck was a Manila galleon, and almost certainly *Santo Cristo de Burgos*, not *San Francisco Xavier*, as previously assumed by many researchers and historians.

According to Indian histories of the wreck, at least some of the crew survived and lived with the local Nehalem and Clatsop Indians for a time. This is significant, because these men would have been the first Europeans the Indians had ever seen. Further, the wreck likely represented the first contact between Europeans and Native Americans on the northern Oregon coast.[3]

It is a mystery how a Spanish ship sailing from the Philippines to Acapulco wound up wrecked so far to the north on the Oregon coast, three hundred miles off course. Now that the focus was on *Santo Cristo*, researchers uncovered and translated a great deal of information about the life of the ship prior to her disappearance. Exactly what happened may never be known. There are clues, however, in the Spanish archives about the Manila trade and *Santo Cristo* that suggest her voyage of 1693 was ill-fated from the start.

Santo Cristo was a ship purpose-built by the Spanish for the long-distance trade between their colonies of Manila in the Philippines and Acapulco in Mexico—a distance of nearly nine thousand miles of open ocean across the North Pacific. From Acapulco, the galleon cargo would be traded to the cities and towns of New Spain, throughout the Americas. These galleons were the largest ships of their day and were built by Spain in the Philippines of native hardwoods, such as teak and *lanang*.

The galleons ranged in size from seven hundred to two thousand tons and were built to undertake voyages of six to nine months, or even longer, and to survive the storms of the North Pacific.

Santo Cristo was built in the royal shipyard at Bagatao Island in Sorsogon Bay in 1687–88 and was considered one of the finest ships ever built in the Philippines at the time. The ship was over 120 feet long, 50 or more feet at the beam, and would have been built with at least three decks in the main hull and a towering sterncastle that rose 40 feet or more above the waterline. It is known from archival records in Spain that *Santo Cristo* normally carried a crew of approximately 230 officers, sailors, soldiers, and gunners. This crew was composed of Spaniards, Filipinos, Malays, and possibly Africans or other Europeans.

Santo Cristo made her first trans-Pacific voyage to Acapulco in 1688. The ship returned to Manila in 1689 and made a second successful voyage to Acapulco in 1690, returning to Manila in 1691. On the 1691 voyage, the viceroy of New Spain in Mexico replaced the commander, Francisco de Arocha, with Don Bernardo Iñiguez del Bayo, a captain of the cavalry. It was not unusual for galleon commanders to be men who had no maritime experience, but who were instead politically connected to someone in power. The viceroy also replaced the sergeant major, boatswain, and master of the ship, causing some discontent in both New Spain and the Philippines.

The reasons for these replacements were, like so many aspects of the Manila galleon trade, purely political and financial. The viceroy wanted one of his associates to be the commander of the galleon, rather than an associate of the governor of Manila. Del Bayo was a Basque nobleman, and as the "general" of the galleon he became the chief officer. Del Bayo was experienced in military and government administration but not in maritime or nautical matters. He was forty-six or forty-seven years old when he was appointed general of *Santo Cristo*.

The voyage west from Acapulco to Manila was the easier of the two legs of the Manila-Acapulco trade. Ships returning to the Philippines primarily carried passengers and silver, and were not heavily overloaded with cargo as were the ships sailing the eastbound leg to Acapulco. The westbound voyage only took three to four months, compared to the six to nine months of the eastbound voyage.[4] Under the command of del Bayo, the westbound voyage to Manila in 1691 was uneventful. The eastbound voyage of 1692, however, was much different.

Santo Cristo had returned to Manila in 1691 too late to make the eastbound voyage to Acapulco that year. The ship sailed for Acapulco on June 30, 1692, with full cargo: an entire year of trade goods for the colony in the form of Asian luxury items. It took the ship almost six weeks to make its way through the islands and straits of the Philippines and into the San Bernardino Strait, arriving there on September 14. This date was relatively late for the sailing season, and put the ship at higher risk for encountering storms in the North Pacific. In early November, *Santo Cristo* was hit by a powerful storm and pushed back toward the Philippines. When the storm had passed, it was noted that the rigging of the foremast was loose. Del Bayo ordered it to be cut away to prevent the mast from falling and damaging the other masts. Somehow, perhaps due to the inexperience of the newly appointed boatswain, the attempt went awry and the foremast fell, taking down the mainmast, which in turn took down the mizzenmast. It took the crew thirteen days to rig a provisional mast and sails, and another three weeks to limp back to the harbor at Naga on the island of Luzon.

It was after the return to the Philippines that the real troubles for del Bayo and his officers began. Only one galleon sailed for Acapulco each year, and that one galleon carried the entire colony's source of income for the year. If the goods did not make it to Acapulco, merchants were bankrupted or put into debt, the Church and the government lost revenue, and widows and orphans of the mariners were left destitute. Failure to make it to Acapulco was the commander general's responsibility. The merchants of Manila, along with the government and the Church, wanted their losses covered.

As *Santo Cristo* underwent repairs to the mast and rigging in Naga, court proceedings against del Bayo and the officers were instituted by the government in Manila. Testimony was taken from officers, crew, and passengers of the ship. The cargo was unloaded and damaged goods were discarded. New cargo was loaded after the repairs had been completed. Del Bayo was cleared of wrongdoing in the return of *Santo Cristo* to the Philippines, but the chief pilot and boatswain were both found responsible and stripped of their rights to work as crew. The chief pilot was permanently banished from the Philippines and the boatswain was exiled from Manila, and therefore prevented from profiting from the galleon trade, for ten years.

The ship was ready to sail for Acapulco in the summer of 1693, but del Bayo was ordered to pay fines and a bond to cover the losses caused by the failure of the 1692 voyage. To avoid paying these, he slipped out of port before the officials from Manila could arrive, and in doing so he left behind a good portion of his supplies and more than thirty of his crew. That means *Santo Cristo* set sail short on supplies and with more than 10 percent of her crew left behind. This was a catastrophic decision for the long and arduous journey east.

It will probably never be known exactly what drove *Santo Cristo* so far north of the regular galleon sailing route or what caused the vessel to wreck at Nehalem. The reason there is so much archival material concerning *Santo Cristo* and her voyage of 1692 is due to the lawsuits filed against del Bayo and the officers of the ship over their return. Information from the Spanish archives verify that the ship was not on an exploration mission, or seeking new harbors, or seeking to plant a new colony. The simplest, and most likely, scenario is that a strong southwest storm pushed *Santo Cristo* to the north and onto the beach at Nehalem. Short of crew, the inexperienced pilot and captain may not have been able to control the ship effectively in a strong storm or keep her off the beach, as they approached an unknown and uncharted coast.

However they wound up on the Oregon coast, the captain and crew of *Santo Cristo* found themselves in an area completely unknown to them. It is possible that they never heard the breakers warning them of a nearby beach if they were in a storm. Some of the Indian accounts of the incident say the ship wrecked in a storm at night, and the next morning the beach was littered with wreckage, cargo, and the bodies of drowned crew members. At least some of the crew managed to survive, making it to the beach despite the frigid water and rough surf of the Oregon coast.

The sight that greeted the local Nehalem Indians on the beach the next morning must have been an amazing one. *Santo Cristo* was a ship larger than any they had ever seen, and one of the largest in the world at that time. The ship carried thousands of tons of cargo and hundreds of strange people who did not look like anyone the Indians had ever met. The survivors from the ship would have known they were among "*los Indios*" of the New World, but of a tribe whose language and customs were completely unknown to them.

Despite the shock of this first meeting, the Nehalem Indians took the survivors in for a time. The Nehalem also salvaged materials from the wreck and incorporated at least some of the goods into their culture, trading beeswax and porcelain up and down the coast as well as inland. Metal tools are found at Indian sites in the area, along with arrowheads and small scrapers fashioned from beautifully flaked shards of Chinese porcelain cups and plates. Beeswax became a widespread trade item along the coast of what is now Oregon and Washington, where it was used as a salve and to make items waterproof.

How long the survivors of the wreck lived with the Nehalem Indians, or whether any of them left the others and attempted to find their way south to Mexico, is unknown. There is no written record of their tales. Nehalem and Clatsop histories of the wreck do tell that after living with the Indians for a period of time, disagreements broke out between the Indians and the survivors. The disagreements came to blows over the survivors' actions toward the Indian women. A fight broke out, and in what is possibly the first account of firearms on the Northwest coast, the Nehalem Indians said the survivors fought by "throwing rocks with great force from under their arms and over their shoulders." The surviving crew members of the Manila galleon were reportedly all killed.

Despite the soured relations that led to the fight between the Indians and the survivors, the event left a strong impression on the coastal Indians, and certainly on any descendants of the crew. The stories of the wreck and the final battle were remembered despite the horrific

Projectile point found at Willapa Bay, Washington, made from porcelain from Santo Cristo.
Courtesy of Lyle Nakonechny

population losses suffered by the coastal Indians in the nineteenth
century, as introduced diseases and forced relocations took their toll and
the Native population declined by as much as 90 percent within a few
generations.

It is likely that survivors of *Santo Cristo* fathered children from their
relationships with Indian women. By the early nineteenth century, there
were Clatsop and Nehalem Indian families whose lineage included
shipwreck survivors from at least the eighteenth century and probably
earlier, and whose descendants had red hair and lighter complexions
than other tribal members. Red hair is a recessive genetic trait, so the
local Indians who possessed red hair must have had European ancestors
on both sides of their families. Contradictory to the oral histories, it is
possible that not all of the survivors were killed, and that some lived out
their lives by being adopted into the local tribes.

Santo Cristo wrecked on the Nehalem beach sometime in the winter
of 1693–94. Six years later, the Oregon coast was rocked by an event

that directly led to the inadvertent preservation of much of the wreck materials. That same event resulted in the deposition of those materials onto the landscape where they could be seen and recovered centuries later by American settlers.

On the evening of January 21, 1700, a very large offshore earthquake struck the Pacific Northwest. The earthquake was a magnitude 9+ and generated a tsunami that was twenty-five feet high. The catastrophic waves carried a large portion of the shipwrecked timbers and cargo over the twenty- to twenty-five-foot-tall foredunes on the seaward side of the Nehalem Spit and into Nehalem Bay. Timbers, beeswax, and porcelain were deposited on the spit and up into the lower Nehalem Valley in a deposit consisting of ocean and river sediment. This deposit was left at elevations above the reach of winter storm waves and tides. The wreck material in the deposit became trapped on land, safe from being washed away by anything other than another large tsunami.

Typically, when a ship wrecks in shallow water near or on the beach, the wreckage is quickly broken up and any parts that float are scattered by wind and waves, leaving very little material behind. This is especially true of wooden sailing ships. Much of their material, such as the hull, sails, and rigging, are easily affected by the elements and quickly rot away. *Santo Cristo*, however, was not like the typical ships of her day. Manila galleons were designed to be incredibly strong. These ships had to be able to survive a year or more in the open ocean and were built out of dense, rot-resistant tropical hardwoods. The tidal range at Nehalem is quite large; with a large, shallow beach, the depth of the water can vary greatly. It is difficult to know exactly where the ship, which would have needed twenty to thirty feet of draft, might have met ground. It is possible the ship grounded offshore, leaving the upper works to be battered by waves, or it may have been carried fairly high on the beach in the storm, leaving portions of the wreck out of reach of all but the largest storm waves.

The deposition of wreck materials by the tsunami at elevations above the reach of waves and tides is what allowed beeswax and timbers to remain in place for centuries after the wreck, rather than washing away.

This in turn allowed the materials to be seen and collected by both the local Indians and the later American settlers, up until the middle of the twentieth century. While much of the beeswax was collected as it was exposed by wind or waves, some residents "mined" for beeswax after figuring out that there was a specific layer within the sand where the beeswax was most commonly found. Early observers thought this layer was a flood deposit, because they did not know large tsunamis had ever struck the coast. Wreck materials are still occasionally found by residents and beachcombers today, usually during construction projects but also sometimes after storms.

It was the abundance of wreck material, particularly the beeswax blocks with their carved symbols and letters, that really caught the imagination of the early settlers and led to the fascination with the wreck and its origins. If the wreck had not been re-deposited by the tsunami, and had instead remained on the beach or in shallow water, it would have dispersed long before Western settlers arrived to write about it. *Santo Cristo* would likely have disappeared into obscurity like many other nearshore wrecks. But it was the sheer abundance of beeswax at Nehalem rather than the presence of timbers or other goods that really caught the attention of everyone, from the first fur traders and passing ship captains to settlers and visitors to the Nehalem area.

So much beeswax was recovered from Nehalem that people hearing about the finds began to question whether it was beeswax at all. Some thought it must be a natural deposit of some kind of petroleum wax. The thought behind this reasoning was that no pre-nineteenth-century ship would carry so many tons of beeswax when it was a relatively inexpensive and widely available commodity by that time. The idea of a ship carrying tons of beeswax with her cargo scattered over so wide an area was unthinkable. By the close of the nineteenth century, the glory days of Spain as a world superpower had faded. The last Manila galleon had sailed in 1815. Large galleons had not been built for generations, and the market that drove Spain to ship such large quantities of beeswax in the seventeenth century no longer existed.

A drilling derrick built at Nehalem in the early twentieth century to drill for oil that was assumed to be the source of the beeswax. **Courtesy of Mark Beach**

The natural petroleum wax idea caused a short-lived oil exploration boom on the north Oregon coast in the late nineteenth century. It was thought that huge oil deposits must be just under the surface. Shares were sold in petroleum companies and drilling rigs were set up. The oil boom was short-lived at Nehalem because there was no oil to be found, and anyone who actually examined the wax could tell that it was, without doubt, beeswax.

The local Nehalem residents likely looked upon the petroleum exploration ventures with a smile. They knew the material was beeswax and from an ancient wreck, even if they did not know the origin of the ship or why she carried such a large cargo of beeswax. Beeswax was found in the form of molded blocks and large candles with wicks. If that was not proof enough, bee parts and even entire bees were melted into the blocks. Additionally, wreckage from the ship, including at least part of the hull, a mast, and a large teak mast-step, could be seen on the spit, and a portion of the ship at the river mouth was exposed at low tide. These sites were often visited by local residents and salvaged for the teak hardwood. This teak was used by the locals to make furniture and walking sticks, and also in the construction of their homes.

The mystery of the ship's origin and destination remained. The fur traders who first wrote of the ship referred to it as "the Spanish ship," but as time passed, speculation on the ship's nationality increased. By the end of the twentieth century, theories pointed to an Asian junk, a Portuguese merchant, or the Manila galleon *San Francisco Xavier*, which left Manila in 1705 and was never seen again. Some researchers even speculated that the mystery ship could have been the wreck of a Dutch pirate ship.

Most serious historians focused on the missing galleon *San Francisco Xavier* as the ship most likely wrecked at Nehalem. She was a good candidate because she went missing late enough to fit with the Indian oral histories of the wreck, and had wrecked after the 1700 tsunami. The galleon was also known to be carrying nearly seventy-five tons of beeswax. Shipwreck artifacts recovered from archaeological sites and examined in private collections all seemed to date to after the Ming dynasty, which ended in the mid-1600s. The only other known missing galleons were from the 1500s, too early to match the artifacts from the Beeswax Wreck.

Building on research conducted since the 1950s on the Beeswax Wreck by Northwest historian Eb Giesecke, the research team partnered with the Geology Department of Portland State University to undertake a geological-based study of the effects of the 1700 tsunami on the Nehalem Spit. The goal of the study was to determine the extent of beach erosion by the tsunami and to identify likely locations for buried post-tsunami wreckage.

As the field research progressed over the next two years, it became clear that the ship had wrecked at Nehalem prior to the tsunami of 1700. Local beachcombers who shared the locations of their finds of porcelain and beeswax were invaluable to the research. The wreck materials and beeswax were deposited in areas where no ocean waves could reach, even if the spit had been eroded by the tsunami. In addition, wreck materials were on or within the tsunami deposit, and not above it.

This was a shocking result for the team. No known but missing galleons fit the date range of the evidence. The ship must have wrecked after the ceramics manufacturing date of 1670 but before the tsunami in 1700. There was one lost galleon, *Santo Cristo de Burgos*, that fit right into the time period. According to modern historians, however, she

A broken fragment of Kangxi porcelain found in the tsunami deposit on Nehalem Spit. **Courtesy of Oregon State Parks**

had burned in the western Pacific in 1693. Faced with this apparent conflict, the research team conducted further study into the archives in Spain to determine the source and details of the historical accounts.

As it turned out, there was no historical documentation of *Santo Cristo* burning in the western Pacific. Instead, Spanish records showed that the ship had left the Philippines in 1693 and was never seen again, despite years of searching for survivors or wreckage both in the western Pacific and on the shores of Central and South America. The story of the ship burning in the western Pacific was found to be a fictional tale, written by an American expatriate living in the Philippines and later mistakenly accepted as fact by the Harvard historian William L. Schurz in his seminal work *The Manila Galleon*, published in 1939.

With the archival proof that *Santo Cristo* had disappeared rather than burned, the mystery of the origin and nationality of the Beeswax Wreck was finally solved. Only one ship fit with the dated material evidence found around Nehalem. It was the Manila galleon *Santo Cristo de Burgos*, sailing from the Philippines to Acapulco in 1693, that had wrecked on the Oregon coast.

It remains a mystery how the galleon came to be so far north of the normal sailing route to Acapulco, and what drove the ship onto the beach. It could have been the inexperienced and incomplete crew. The galleon had been assigned a new and unseasoned captain, inexperienced pilots, and a young boatswain. *Santo Cristo* also was missing over 10 percent of her crew after her rushed departure from the Philippines. The ship could have had structural problems, as the masts had been damaged and repaired the previous year. A huge storm could have blown the ship far north. It could have been a combination of these factors, or something else altogether. *Santo Cristo* seemed to have had a run of bad luck, despite her early promise as being the finest ship built in the Philippines to that date. It is perhaps no surprise the vessel wound up wrecking on a then-unknown shore.

The wreck is known because of the remarkable oral histories of the local Nehalem and Clatsop Indians, the meticulous Spanish record keeping, the eyewitness accounts of wreckage from early settlers, and

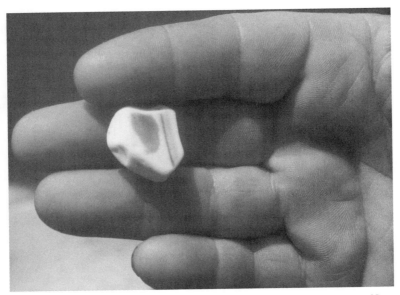

Fragments of porcelain are still occasionally found by beachcombers in the area. **Courtesy of Scott Williams**

from the materials that were salvaged from the wreck over the past three hundred years. These materials can still be seen in many of the city and county museums of coastal Oregon. The excitement and intrigue surrounding the wreck continues to this day as beachcombers continue to find bits of beeswax, broken fragments of exotic Chinese porcelain, and fragments of Asian stoneware jars on the beaches around Nehalem.

While the identity of the Beeswax Wreck seems to have been solved, the final resting place of the ship remains a mystery. Additional archaeological work may tell whether the lower hull rests in the shallows off Nehalem Spit or if the vessel broke up on the cliffs of Neahkahnie Mountain, scattering its cargo across a wide swath of sea bottom. Research on the site may show whether the tsunami of 1700 lifted the ship completely out of the shallows and deposited the wreckage on Nehalem Spit, or tore the upper decks off and left the lower hull behind. Only time will tell.

Scott Williams

USS *SHARK*

STRANDED NAVY VESSEL IN CONTESTED OREGON COUNTRY, 1846

I don't think it's wood, Dad. It's rusting," Miranda said. Miranda Petrone and her father were walking along the beach in Arch Cape, Oregon. The storms that winter had scraped vast amounts of sand from the coastline, and there were also unusually low tides that Presidents' Day weekend in 2008. Her father had thought they were standing by an unusual-looking wooden stump. In fact, they had rediscovered two lost cannons from the navy schooner USS *Shark*.

The American borders of the Pacific Northwest were not yet established when *Shark* wrecked near the mouth of the Columbia River in 1846. The story of the *Shark* helps us understand how the northern and western boundaries of the United States were established as well as illuminates the history of the fledgling American Navy.

Shark was one of four similar vessels designed by renowned ship constructor William Doughty for the US Navy in 1820. Each of the four was assigned to be built by different shipyards along the eastern seaboard: *Alligator* at the Boston Navy Yard, *Dolphin* at the Philadelphia Navy Yard, *Porpoise* at the Portsmouth Navy Yard, and *Shark*, which

USS Shark, *print from watercolor.* **Courtesy of the Columbia River Maritime Museum, Astoria**

came out of the Washington Navy Yard on May 17, 1821. Of the Baltimore clipper design, these topsail schooners were fast and of relatively shallow draft, making them ideal for chasing down pirates in the islands of the Caribbean and for intercepting slave-carrying ships off the west coast of Africa. They were eighty-six feet in length; twenty-four feet, nine inches in breadth; and had a depth of hold of ten feet, four inches.

The schooner displaced 198 tons and carried a complement of around seventy officers and crew to man her. This was considerably less than the larger ships of the navy and therefore less expensive to build, operate, and maintain. Construction of *Shark* cost $23,627.

Lieutenant Matthew C. Perry was twenty-seven years old when he was ordered to the first command of *Shark* and put in charge of making preparations for her first cruise. (Later, in 1853 at the age of fifty-nine, Perry played a leading role in the opening of Japan to foreign trade.) *Shark* took on board Dr. Eli Ayers and escorted him to the west coast of Africa in order to establish a colony there for freed slaves, which became known as Liberia. A year later, in 1822, *Shark* was ordered to the West

Indies Squadron for the purpose of suppressing piracy and the slave trade in and around the Caribbean. In her first two years, *Shark* was directly or in part responsible for the capture of several pirate vessels, including the *Bandera de Sangre*, which translates as "Banner of Blood."

Under various commanders from 1826 to 1832, *Shark* cruised off the west coast of Africa to suppress the slave trade across the Atlantic. The United States Congress and the Parliament of the United Kingdom each ratified an act in 1807 that prohibited the importation of slaves and the trafficking in slaves, respectively. Although it did little to end slavery, it did deter the international trade of human slaves and imposed fines on ship captains who continued the practice. From 1833 to 1838, again under various commanders, *Shark* patrolled the Mediterranean and was engaged once again in pirate suppression.

In 1839 the schooner *Shark* was ordered to the Pacific Squadron under the command of Lieutenant Abraham Bigelow and became the first US warship to pass through the Straits of Magellan from east to west. Once in the Pacific she protected US interests in South America and along the California coast, which belonged to Mexico at the time. The Secretary of the Navy noted in 1841 that "all who witnessed the operations of *Shark* were inspired with increased respect for the American flag."

Since the establishment of Astoria on the Columbia River in 1811, claim to the large area of the Pacific Northwest known at that time as the Oregon Country had been under dispute. The region was under joint occupation by Great Britain and the United States. Great Britain was represented by the Hudson's Bay Company, which was heavily invested in the fur trade. The foothold of the United States in the region was bolstered by a large influx of emigrants arriving by wagon trains into the valleys of the watershed south of the Columbia River in the 1840s.

Political uncertainty and pressures on existing resources increased tensions between the two nations, and some began to talk of war to settle the issues. Establishment of the northern boundary was in contention. Britain wanted the Columbia River to be the border, while many in the US shouted "Fifty-four forty or fight!" to push for a boundary above the fifty-fourth parallel, lobbying for the 1844 election of presidential candidate James Polk and his expansionist policies.

Shark was sent into this tense atmosphere in 1846. Under the command of Lieutenant Neil Howison, the navy schooner was ordered first to Honolulu for repairs and preparations for a voyage up the Columbia River to Fort Vancouver. While in the river *Shark* was "to obtain correct information of that country and to cheer our citizens in that region by the presence of the American flag." Before leaving Honolulu, Lieutenant Howison conferred with two captains who had recently been to the Columbia River. Both said the shoals at the mouth had changed greatly in recent years. The information was invaluable. Howison only had "a copy of a copy, upon tracing paper, of Wilkes's chart, which was even now, before its publication, out of date." Lieutenant Charles Wilkes had been in the Columbia with the US Exploring Expedition in 1841. Despite having sounded the river in great detail, he lost the vessel *Peacock* on the bar in an area now known as Peacock Spit.

On July 18, 1846, *Shark* neared the mouth of the Columbia River and assessed the entrance. Howison was gravely concerned about this passage. He later reported, "I cannot deny that I felt sensibly the weight of my responsibilities." It did not help that a sailor from his crew who had been on *Peacock* mentioned it was the five-year anniversary of the wreck.

"About 10 o'clock a.m., of July 18, I anchored in ten fathoms, Cape Disappointment bearing NE. by N., distant five miles," Howison recalled. "Several guns were fired and signals made for a pilot; but seeing no one moving about the shore, on either side of the river, I took the master with me in the whale-boat, and pulled in the channel, between the breakers, sounding in no less than four fathoms, and passing sufficiently far in to recognise the landmarks on the north shore, described in Wilkes's sailing directions."

After returning to the ship, with the wind from the west and a flood tide, they smoothly glided the navy schooner safely into Baker Bay to the relief of everyone on board. A boat soon came alongside with three Americans on board to welcome the vessel: William H. Gray of Clatsop

Plains, a missionary named H. H. Spaulding, and A. L. Lovejoy, who was the mayor of Oregon City.

With no regular pilots engaged on the river, the three men recommended the services of James D. Sauls to pilot the ship to Astoria. Sauls was a black sailor who had been stranded in the area when *Peacock* wrecked five years before. Unfortunately, twenty minutes after Sauls took the helm, the ship ran aground on Chinook Spit. Sauls was listed as a cook on *Peacock*. His piloting experience was not documented in the historical record. The navy vessel was stuck fast until the change of tide later that night. Undamaged, the ship anchored in the channel.

While the ship was stuck, the three Americans had returned to Astoria to engage the services of another man to pilot the ship to Astoria. They felt partly responsible for having recommended Sauls. Alexander Lattie was the chief factor of Fort George for the Hudson's Bay Company. With the help of Lattie, the vessel finally arrived safely in Astoria the next morning.

Howison spent the next few days exploring the Clatsop Plains. He visited with settlers in the area and brought fresh food on board. The ship was "abundantly furnished by the American settlers here with fresh beef and vegetables."

On July 22, after consulting with Lattie and an Indian named George, who was familiar with the river upstream from Astoria, *Shark* departed for Fort Vancouver, arriving there two days later on July 24. The voyage up the river was tortuous and slow. A small boat from the ship had to travel out in front the entire way, casting a lead line to sound the depths of the channel.

Once they arrived at Fort Vancouver, they were greeted by Her Britannic Majesty's sloop-of-war HBM *Modeste*, under the command of Captain Thomas Baillie. The ships kept close watch on each other. The actions of the officers and crew aboard *Shark* were well documented in the log of *Modeste*. Neither party wished to inflame tensions between the Americans and the British, so both crews were on their best behavior during the visit.

Howison went up to Oregon City and took a week to explore the Willamette Valley on horseback. He was accompanied by the provisional governor, George Abernethy, as his guide. Meanwhile the first lieutenant, Mr. W. S. Schenck, was sent up the Columbia as far as The Dalles to make military observations, a practice known as reconnoitering. *Shark* discovered that much of what had already been reported about Oregon Country by Wilkes and others was factual and fair and that it was likely to fulfill its great promise as an agricultural and economic asset to the United States.

Skilled labor was much in demand and opportunities to make a living were readily available, so many of the crew were tempted to desert. As many as ten went missing. Only two were retrieved during their short six weeks in the area.

Under orders to depart the river by September 1, Howison and crew left Fort Vancouver on the morning of August 23, cautiously winding their way down the Columbia aboard *Shark*. Just under five miles downstream they came upon the American bark *Toulon*, bound for the Hawaiian Islands, then still commonly referred to as the Sandwich Islands, hard aground on a sandbar in the middle of the channel.[1] *Shark* came alongside and offered assistance, and spent three days trying to help free *Toulon* from the sandbar, with eventual success.

Battling constant headwinds, they finally got back to Baker Bay just inside the mouth of the river on September 8, already seven days overdue. Howison spent the next day observing the bar and making preparations for the crossing. On the afternoon of September 10, he attempted to cross out over the bar. The following is an account of those dramatic events described in a letter and statement submitted by Howison and later recounted by Norman Howerton in an article published in the *Oregon Historical Quarterly*.

> The Schooner *Shark* cleared Cape Disappointment and stood
> down the north channel on a line of bearing that kept Green
> Point open with Cape Disappointment. Lieutenant Howison,

commanding, was on the quarterdeck, keeping his vessel in position. He stationed a passed midshipman on the lee side to observe when the schooner arrived at a point where Coxcomb Hill would be a ship's length open with Point Adams. Those bearings should have brought *Shark* to the center of the South Clatsop channel in about four fathoms of water, according to the Wilkes chart, made five years before.

Hauling on the wind to pass out to sea, *Shark* was forced into the south breakers. Lieutenant Howison quickly tacked ship to northward, but the tide hung on the weather bow and brought the breakers on Middle Sands directly ahead. Tacking ship again to the south, he found *Shark* slipping rapidly to leeward. The anchor was let go in an attempt to hold the schooner, but the chain snapped like a thread.

The ship fought against the strong tide in the breakers, but struck the sandbar. *Shark* was stuck. Howison gave the order to begin an evacuation of the ship with the smaller boats. One member of the crew, Burr Osborn, later described the scene.

> Our boats consisted of the Captain's gig, a whale boat, first cutter and launch. The gig was the first boat loaded with the ship papers and the sick with the surgeon. The roll of the vessel brought the fluke of the anchor in contact with the boat and stove her all to pieces, but through the precaution of the captain in ordering all the ends of the running rigging to be thrown overboard, the boat's crew and the sick managed to get hold of a rope and were all saved. During this time, every breaker broke clear over the vessel and continued doing so until ebb tide, when we lowered our other boats without damage.

Upon making their way out of the breakers and onto Clatsop Beach, some members of the crew built a fire out of timbers from the wreckage of *Peacock* while they waited. The small boats were to return for the rest of the men when the changing tides made it safe to do so. The *Oregon Historical Quarterly* detailed the long night spent on board for the rest of the crew.

> Lieutenant Schenck, Midshipman Davidson and twenty-one men remained aboard *Shark* with Lieutenant Howison. The masts were cut away, hoping the vessel would hold together until the rescue boats returned. At one A.M., *Shark* was completely waterlogged. The flood tide gradually crowded Lieutenant Howison and his men into narrow limits, until the bowsprit and the top of the two quarterdeck houses were the only inhabitable spots on the ship. Occasionally heavy swells broke over the men with terrific force, even on their last places of refuge, and Lieutenant Howison ordered everyone secured to the vessel by a cord passed around him. It was a precaution that may have saved several lives.
>
> In the early hours of the morning, just before dawn, the ebbing tide meeting the ocean swell, again caused heavy break that lashed furiously over and about *Shark*. But the dawn brought the return of the boats and the men were relieved from their perilous situation. Lieutenant Howison was the last man to leave the ill-fated vessel.

The fully assembled crew made their way to Astoria, exposed to the cold, damp Northwest air. Burr Osborn described the nascent town as having "three log houses and one small frame house." It would not be enough to house some seventy crew members of *Shark*. He said the log houses belonged to the Hudson's Bay Company and two of them were empty, used by trappers bringing furs to sell. Osborn had just joined the crew four months earlier, when *Shark* stopped in Hawaii. He had been on the crew of a whaler and was stranded there.

Lieutenant Howison immediately set about providing for the welfare of his crew. "Cast on shore as we were, with nothing besides the clothes we stood in," he said, "and those thoroughly saturated, no time was to be lost seeking new supplies. I left the crew, indifferently sheltered at Astoria, and, with the purser in company, pushed up the river to Vancouver, whither news of our disaster had preceded us, and elicited the sympathy and prompt attentions of the factors of the Hudson's Bay Company and of Captain Baillie and the officers of her Britannic Majesty's ship *Modeste*."

The British had in fact loaded a boat with all the necessary supplies for relief and sent it down the river before Lieutenant Howison arrived. It was a gesture he was most grateful for, but nevertheless politely refused. Instead, he purchased what he needed at Vancouver. Upon his return to Astoria, he had the crew set about building suitable shelters, as they were uncertain when they would be able to leave. These shelters, known as "Sharkville," were later used by emigrants while they waited for their own homes to be constructed.

In addition to providing for their survival, Lieutenant Howison had the men constantly exploring the beaches, looking for usable remains of their vessel. Local Indians were also harvesting the useful copper and iron fastenings from the planks littering the shoreline. Tribal members reported that a large portion of the hull with three guns attached had come ashore some twenty to thirty miles south of the wreck site. Midshipman Simes was sent to investigate. He confirmed three carronades, a capstan, and a cleat with some links of chain had washed up on the beach. Carronades were short, large-caliber cannons used on naval vessels. He attempted to pull the guns up farther on the beach but only managed to get one gun out of the surf. He reported back to Howison, who passed the information on to Provisional Governor Abernethy, with the hope that he might be able to arrange retrieval of the armaments at a later date.

These objects from *Shark* have lent their names to various landmarks in the area: Shark Creek, Cannon Beach, and even Shark Rock in Astoria, where crewmen carved their fate, and supposedly names, into the stone for posterity. Howison reported, "Within a month all the upper works, decks, sides and spars came ashore from the wreck, but separated

Shark Rock was on display in Astoria at the intersection of Eighth and Niagara Streets for many years before being brought to the museum. **Courtesy of the Columbia River Maritime Museum, Astoria**

a distance of 75 miles from each other, and were of no value, from the long wash and chafing which they had undergone."

Just over a month after the wreck, on October 11, the crew was cheered by the sight of a sail just offshore. The Hudson's Bay Company schooner *Cadboro*, recently from Vancouver Island, had entered the river and was headed up to Fort Vancouver. Lieutenant Howison had some of his officers look over the *Cadboro* to determine if it might be suitable to carry their crew. The vessel was only fifty-seven feet long, but they determined that it would suit their needs, so he wasted no time going ahead to Fort Vancouver to charter the vessel.

On November 16 the American bark *Toulon*, which the crew of the *Shark* had helped free from a sandbar back in August, returned from Hawaii with news. The Oregon Treaty had put an end to the border dispute with the British. The land below the forty-ninth parallel, which forms the northern edge of what is now known as Washington State, with the exception of where it dips south around the tip of Vancouver Island in British Columbia, now belonged to the United States. The tension at the northern border that *Shark* had been sent to alleviate was no longer an issue. In fact, the treaty had been signed by President Polk on June 15, which was over a month before *Shark* first arrived at the mouth of the Columbia River. The United States had also been at war with Mexico since April over the southern border. On the Pacific Coast, the United States had taken possession of San Francisco, which is where the crew made plans to head so they could rejoin the US Navy.[2]

"This intelligence rendered us doubly anxious to escape from our idle imprisonment in the river, and we seized upon the first day of sunshine to embark," Howison reported. Eager to get under way, the officers and crew from *Shark* boarded the smaller schooner, *Cadboro*, to take them to San Francisco, where they could be redeployed to help with the Mexican-American War. They made it past Astoria and anchored the next day in Baker Bay on the north side of the river just inside the treacherous bar at the mouth. As they waited for favorable crossing conditions, the winter stormy season rolled in, as it does every November. The crew would be stuck there by harsh wind and weather for six more weeks. "We suffered very much from our crowded stowage in this small craft," Howison reported. "The weather was wet and cold; and the vessel not affording the comfort of stove or fireplace, and without space for exercise."

While stranded inside the bar, *Toulon* made it back down to join *Cadboro*. Together they set sail for San Francisco on January 18 of 1847, exactly six months after *Shark* had first anchored outside the river on the other side of Cape Disappointment from Baker Bay. The crew finally arrived in San Francisco later that month on January 27, where they were reassigned to two other US Navy vessels in the area.

Their assignment in the Oregon Territory on the Columbia River had lasted months longer than intended. The area where they had spent the fall and much of the winter was now decisively part of the United States. Upon hearing the news of the treaty with Great Britain, Lieutenant Howison sent a proud letter to Governor Abernethy with a parcel. "One of the few articles preserved from the shipwreck of the late United States schooner *Shark* was her stand of colors," he wrote. "I do myself the honor of transmitting the flags (an ensign and union-jack) to your address; nor can I omit the occasion to express my gratification and pride that this relic of my late command should be emphatically the first *United States* flag to wave over the undisputed and purely American territory of Oregon."

The remnants of *Shark* remained on the coastline of Oregon, occasionally peeking out of the sand. Fifty-two years after the wreck, in 1898, one of the three carronades midshipman Simes had attempted to pull out of the surf was noticed by a passerby, John Hobson. He and some associates managed to pull it up onto dry land along with the capstan and a cleat. It remained on public display, out in the elements, for over ninety-one years. During that time many of the pieces disappeared, leaving only the carronade and the capstan. Fearing further vandalism and deterioration, they were taken indoors by representatives from the Clatsop County Historical Society and put on display in their local museum in Astoria. A bell from *Shark* also ended up with the Clatsop County Historical Society. Eventually the community named after the carronade built a suitable museum, the Cannon Beach History Center and Museum, and raised the money to conserve and stabilize the badly weathered carronade and capstan. They are now safely on display at the museum.

In 2008, 162 years after the wreck, the remaining two carronades were rediscovered along the same beach on Presidents' Day by the young girl and her father, who were visiting the coast. It had been an especially stormy winter. Much of the beach sand along the northern Oregon coast had been scoured away, revealing many interesting objects. The two large concreted "blobs" were reported to local officials, who contacted the Oregon Parks and Recreation Department. The department swiftly secured the objects, dragging them up farther onto the beach out of the surf, just as Simes had tried to do in 1846. The state archaeologist was notified, and a park ranger remained on-site all night to keep an eye on the finds.

Because the objects were discovered on state land, Oregon state authorities were put in charge of the operation. The Oregon Beach Bill of 1967 had made all beaches state property from the first dune to the sea as a way of ensuring public access to the entire coastline. If swift action was not taken, these two artifacts would once again be hidden by the sea and sand.

On Tuesday, the state archaeologist, joined by representatives of the Columbia River Maritime Museum, stood on the beach answering questions from the press. The two carronades and their mounts were carefully removed with the aid of a backhoe to waiting tubs of water provided by the Nehalem Bay State Park staff. After several hours of working against the elements and the tides, the state park crew was successful in getting the two pieces off the beach and into the tubs on the truck, ready for transport to the maintenance facility at the park.

Because these objects had been in a saturated marine environment for so long, they needed to be kept wet to prevent deformity from rapid dehydration of the organic elements and oxidation of the metal. They remained in the tubs for about a year while plans were made for their conservation and preservation. The park allowed viewing of the

Carronade in the sand at Arch Cape before removal for preservation. **Courtesy of the Columbia River Maritime Museum, Astoria**

State archaeologist Dennis Griffin speaking to the press on February 19, 2008.

carronades for special school groups and tours during this time, sharing the story and history of *Shark*. While at the park, portable equipment was brought in and X-rays were taken of the concreted blobs. The scans revealed wonderfully intact carronades inside, with their wooden mounts still attached.

A committee composed of state and federal officials, museum representatives, and community stakeholders met to discuss plans for the carronades. Ultimately it was decided to send them to the Conservation Research Laboratory at Texas A&M University for treatment.

The US Navy was also brought into the conversation. The Sunken Military Craft Act of 2004 protects military shipwrecks worldwide, "including equipment, cargo, as well as remains and personal effects of the crew and passengers within the craft and its debris field." Any material recovered from military vessels throughout the world are still the property of the navy for the country to which it belonged. In the case of the carronades, the US Navy agreed with the recommendation of the committee, and arrangements for transport to Texas were made.

In 2009 the two concreted carronades were delivered to the Conservation Research Laboratory in Texas. The first step in their conservation was to remove the concreted material from around the two guns. This was done with pneumatic needle guns, picks, chisels, hammers, and even delicate dental tools. Once the bulk of the accreted sand, rock, and debris was removed, the organic elements were separated from the inorganic elements for their respective treatments. The cast-iron guns and associated hardware were put into tanks with a special solution and connected to a low-voltage electrical source so that the rusted metal, the iron oxides, could be reduced back into iron by driving off the oxygen that had bonded chemically with the iron, forming the rust. This process took five years to complete. Meanwhile, organic materials such as wood, rope fibers, and feathers had been separated from the concretion. They were treated separately using silicone oil and various solvents in order to clean and stabilize them.

Interestingly, when the outer layer of material was removed and the carronades were separated from their wooden mounts, it was revealed

State officials and archaeologists examine the carronade at the Nehalem Bay State Park maintenance building after removal from the beach at Arch Cape. **Courtesy of Nehalem Bay State Park**

that one of the guns bore maker's marks indicating it was of British manufacture. Research identified it as having been cast at the Wiggin & Graham foundry in England around 1805. How it came to be on board an American naval ship is still a mystery, but it is known that at the time *Shark* was launched in 1821, many British guns were in the inventory of the US Navy.

While the carronades were being treated in Texas, the committee debated over who was best able to provide for the ongoing care of these relics from the past. Due to the long period of time in a marine environment, the wood material, although intact, now lacked the structural integrity to support the 1,200 pounds of each of the guns. In order to display them in proper position, replica slides and mounts would have to be made.

Ultimately the Columbia River Maritime Museum was chosen as the preferred curation facility, having the space, staff, and means to display both of the remaining guns from *Shark*. They were unveiled in a special gallery designed for them in 2014. Shark Rock, where the crewman had carved "The Shark was lost Sept 16, 1846," is on display in the museum

Restored carronades on display at the Columbia River Maritime Museum. **Courtesy of the Columbia River Maritime Museum, Astoria**

along with the carronades. The exhibit has been seen by over one hundred thousand museum visitors every year since the gallery opened. The harrowing tale of the US schooner *Shark* at the mouth of the Columbia River and her role in the establishment of the Oregon Territory continues to capture the imagination of current and future generations.

Jeff Smith

DESDEMONA

NAMESAKE FROM THE
OREGON TERRITORY, 1857

On the cold New Year's Eve night of 1856, the American bark *Desdemona* approached the mouth of the Columbia River along the rocky coast. The mouth of the river has always been a perilous bar, with powerful currents, steep breaking waves, and dangerous shallow sandbars. The town of Astoria, offering safety and warmth, was less than fifteen miles away.

The crew was familiar with the passage. *Desdemona* made regular runs between San Francisco and the Oregon Territory, bringing much-needed goods to a growing American population. Many of the local settlers were pioneers who had made the difficult overland journey from the East following a different sort of tide. They had traveled with the dusty overland covered wagon trains on the Oregon Trail.

A brand-new lighthouse had gone into service just two months earlier, on October 15, 1856. It stood atop Cape Disappointment on the northern headlands of the entrance to the Columbia River. During the first US Coastal Survey of the Oregon Territory, conducted by Lieutenant Commander William P. McArthur six years earlier, McArthur spoke of the need for a lighthouse, and he requested five buoys to mark the channel for Euro-American ships. "The greatly increasing commerce of Oregon demands that these improvements be made immediately," he wrote.

The Cape Disappointment Lighthouse stands on a headland 220 feet above the water. The beacon had to be low enough not to be hidden by the fog that frequently lingered at the treetops. At the same time, it had to be high enough for ships to spot from twenty miles or more out at sea. The local people, the Chinook, called the area *Kah'eese*. They had long used the headlands as an observation post before Europeans and Americans began to visit the area regularly by ship.

In 1775, Spanish explorer Bruno de Heceta called the cliffs *Cabo de San Rogue*. British merchant John Mears renamed it Cape Disappointment in 1788. Neither went far enough upriver to learn whether it was indeed a mighty river or just a bay. It was an American, Captain Robert Gray, who finally maneuvered his ship upriver in 1792. He tried to rename the rocky sea cliffs Cape Hancock, but the name did not stick. Lewis and Clark used the British name Cape Disappointment in their journals.

When the lighthouse to help guide ships was being built in 1853, the bark *Oriole*, carrying materials to help build the tower, was herself wrecked at the base of the cliff. The Fresnel lighthouse lens was finally lit up in 1856 for ships like *Desdemona* to more easily locate the river approach.

Desdemona was a sailing bark of the West Coast trade, carrying passengers and freight from San Francisco up to Astoria and along the Columbia River inland to Portland. On the return trip, the ship often carried Northwest lumber down to San Francisco, where it was needed for the population boom of the gold rush. *Desdemona* had been built in Jonesboro, Maine, in 1847 by Josiah Holmes Jr. & Brother. The three-masted ship measured 104 feet long with a width of 26 feet at the widest part, known as the beam. She had a hold depth of 12 feet 7 inches.

When the ship first arrived in Oregon, it was owned by Abernethy & Clark, based in Oregon City. George C. Abernethy was a well-known successful businessman in the region who controlled one of the first newspapers in Oregon, *The Spectator*. He had come to the West to help

THE
ENTIRE CARGO
OF THE
Bark Desdemona,

Consisting of a large and extensive assortment of Merchandise, adapted to the wants of this country, is now opened, and will be offered for sale, at the re-fitted warehouse of Geo. Abernethy & Co., at

WHOLESALE & RETAIL.

The Assortment consists of the following articles, viz:

Assorted Calicoes, Muslin de Lains, Alpaccas, Paramattas, Black and Changeable Silks, Bonnet Silk, Assorted Lawns, Laces, Edgings, Insertings, Ribbons, Muslin Collars, Silk Cravats, Ladies' Neck Ties, Black Silk Mantillas, Silk Shawls, Wool Shawls, Black Cassimere Shawls, Barege Shawls, Broche Shawls, Thibet Long Shawls, Ladies and Gentlemen's assorted Cotton, Silk and Kid Gloves, assorted Veils, Black Bombazines, Ginghams, Plaid Mohair Lustre, Colored Cambrics, Swiss Muslin, Curtain Muslin, Irish Linens, Table Covers, Lancaster Quilts, Red, Blue, Yellow and White Flannel, Printed Flannel, Linen Damask Table

Cloths, Bird's Eye Diaper, Russia and Scotch Diaper, Strainer Cloths, Shirting, Sheetings, Blue Drills, Plain Drilling, Bed Ticking, Plaid Linseys, Gala Plaid, Twilled Bagging, Clalifornia Stripe, Cot. Batting, White and Black Wadding, 2¼ Bus. Bags, Kentucky Jeans, Cassimeres, Satinetts, Broadcloths, Silk and Cotton Velvet, Wool Carpeting, Stair Carpeting, Hearth Rugs, Draggets, Linen and Cotton Thread, Mack'w Blankets, White, Blue and Scarlet, Fine Family Blankets, White, Blue, Mix'd Grey and Scarlet Knitting Yarn, Knitting Cotton, Rob Roy, Woollen Socks, Cotton Hose.

A Large Assortment of Ready Made Clothing.

Cut and Wrought Nails, Log and Trace Chains, C. S. Nail Hammers, Setts Planes, Moulding and Brace Planes, Iron and Steel Squares, Braces and Bitts, Drawing Knives, Spoke Shaves, Hand Saws, Panel Saws, Buck Saws, Cross-Cut Saws, Mill Saws, Carpenters' Adzes, assorted Augers, Jack Planes, Socket, Firmer and Framing Chisels, Carpenters' Rules, Bench Hatchets, Broad Axes, Chopping Axes, Brass, Cast and Wrought Butts, Hand Vices, Compasses, Spirit Levels, Oil Stones, Knob Locks, Plate Locks, Chest Locks, Pad Locks, Till Locks, Trunk Locks, Gun Locks, Handsaw Files, Bastard Files, Mill Files, Horse Rasps, Steelyards and Spring Balances, Grain, Grass and Brush Scythes, Iron and Steel Shovels and Spades, Wool Cards, Grind Stones with Cranks and Rollers, Cast and Brass And-

irons, Counter Scales, 7–9, 8–10, 10–12 Window Glass, Window Sash, Coffee Mills, Blacksmiths' Anvils, Vices, Dies, Sledge Hammers and Bellows, Plows, Crowbars, Cast Iron Scrapers, Hay Forks and Rakes, Brass and Brittannia Candlesticks, Shoe Nails, Shoemakers' Hammers, Knives, Pincers and Foot Rules, Bed Screws, Door Bolts, Shovels and Tongs, Shot, Sail Twine, Clothes Lines, Bed Cords, Shoe Thread, Tea Trays, Knitting Needles, Shears, Scissors, Brass, Steel and Silver Thimbles, Brick Trowels, Compass Saws, Cow Bells, Tea Bells, Hand Bells, Saws, Mouse Traps, Paint Brushes, Shoe Brushes, Dust Brushes, Cloth Brushes, Hand Bellows, Cooking and Parlor Stoves, Side Saddles, Saddles, Bridles, Harness, Whips, Halters, Saddle-Bags, Riding Whips.

A Complete Stock of Ladies', Gentlemen's and Childrens' Boots and Shoes.

Sugar, Tea, Coffee, Molasses, Crush'd Sugar, Pow'd Sugar, Honey, Stewart's Syrup, Vinegar, Saleratus, Bar Soap, White Soap, Castile Soap, Fancy Soap, Pepper, All-spice, Ginger, Beeswax, Mustard, Sweet Oil, Nutmegs, Cloves, Starch, Snuff, Sperm Oil, Candles, Rice, Dried Apples, Dried Peaches, Coarse Turk's Island Salt, Fine Table Salt, Tobacco, Tapioca, Sago, Cream Tartar, Soda, Pipes, Blacking, Linseed Oil, Turpentine, Varnish. China Tea Setts, Edwards' Iron Stone Crockery, Yellow Iron Stone-ware, Glassware, Solar Lamps, Wood-seat Chairs,

Cane-seat Chairs, Rocking Chairs, Nurse Chairs, Spring-seat Sofas, Bureaus with Mirrors, Bedsteads, Mattrasses, Comforters, Cots, Wooden Buckets, Pails, Well Buckets, Wash Boards, Tubs, Nests Measures, Brooms. Castor Oil, Hebbard's Pills, Hot Drops, Composition Opodeldoc, Paregoric, Tonic Lobelia, Camphor, Reck's Bitters for Coughs, Bayberry, Liniment, Ointment, Essence Peppermint, Cinnamon, Wintergreen, Sassafras, Hemlock and Spearmint, Sarsaparilla, &c., &c., &c.

OREGON CITY, NOV. 12, 1850.

SPECTATOR PRINT.—OREGON CITY.

Advertisement to sell cargo from Desdemona *from the Abernethy warehouse.* Oregon Spectator, *1850.* **Courtesy of the Oregon Historical Society**

bolster American settlement and the work of the Methodist missionaries who were intent on converting the Native peoples to Christianity.[1] The concept of Manifest Destiny, a belief that US expansion throughout North America was an inevitable God-given right, had become popular in the mid-nineteenth century.

Abernethy holds the distinction of being the first governor of Oregon. As governor, he advocated for the establishment of a pilot service to help ships cross the Columbia River Bar. As a businessman, he saw the value of a safe, steady stream of trade goods in and out of the region. He was elected to serve the first self-organized government of Oregon Country until the land officially became part of the United States, as the Oregon Territory, in 1848. Oregon Country was a disputed region whose primary export had been the fur trade, mostly promoted and financed by Americans, the British, and the French.

A pilot service was successfully organized in 1846. Before the Columbia River Bar pilots were established, local Clatsop or Chinook tribal members were sometimes hired to guide ships safely across the bar or up into the river toward Portland and Fort Vancouver. They were experts at maneuvering around the tricky shoals of the Columbia River. The Clatsops lived in the area south of the river, the northwest corner of what is today the state of Oregon, while the Chinook were on the north side of the river, or southwest Washington State today.

When *Desdemona* arrived in the Oregon Territory filled with goods, full-page advertisements invited locals to purchase from a wide variety of goods at the wharf. One manifest boasted 10 casks and 32 cases of ale, 45 casks and 67 cases of porter, 93 bags of arrowroot, 444 sacks of rice, 57 tons of coal, 253 mattresses, 338 pillows, and 732 bags of coffee. On the return journey to San Francisco, the ship carried lumber and agricultural goods. The *Daily Alta California* reported one arrival of *Desdemona* in San Francisco carrying 186,000 board-feet of lumber. The journey had taken six days from Astoria.

Seth Luen Pope was a crew member on *Desdemona*. He had been in the Northwest for two years and kept a daily diary detailing the weather and ocean conditions, repurposing the pages of an account book into

For Portland, Oregon.

FIRST VESSEL.

On SATURDAY, September 24th, 1855.

 The fast sailing barque

DESDEMONA,

FARLEY, master,

Will take passengers and freight at the lowest rates.

Apply to the Captain, on board, at Simpson & Jackson's Wharf, Stewart street, or to

D. C. M. GOODSELL, Shipwright,

Beal street,

s20 3   Between Mission and Market.

Evening News copy.

NUMEROUS IMITATIONS OF EXTRACT DE ABSINTHE, of the ED. PERNOD BRAND, having lately been introduced in this market, the undersigned would inform the public that the necessary steps have been taken to prevent fresh fraud and imposition for the future. In the meantime, purchasers of this article will do well to look to the cork, which on the genuine article is covered with a green seal, showing the initials E. P.

RUTTE & CO.,

104 Battery street

Sole Agents for EDWARD PERNOD, for California and Oregon.   s20 1w

Desdemona *advertisement,* Daily Alta California, *1855.*

what he titled the "Journal log of a voyage from Oak Point W.T. [Washington Territory] on barque Desdemona to San Francisco by S.L. Pope of St. Helens—Oregon Territory 1855." In late November, off the southern Oregon coast, he reported "bad cross sea causing the vessle [*sic*] to roll heavily the Barrells [*sic*] in the half deck got adrift and were' obliged to coil rope between them." The seas lessened by morning and he went on to say, "Ends pleasant had the forenoon watch below 'turned in and had a first-rate Nap."

Winter storms during the rainy season off the Oregon coast were unpredictable. Sudden localized storms called squalls often popped up, whipping ship sails with high winds and heavy rains. Ocean swells battered the wooden ships constantly. The life of a nineteenth-century mariner was not for those with weak dispositions.

On the last day of 1856, *Desdemona* was carrying a cargo of general merchandise bound for Astoria. Astoria had just incorporated as a city earlier that year, and there were fewer than five hundred residents in the city and surrounding Clatsop County at the time. It was cold for the holidays that year, below freezing in most spots.

Seth Pope had left the ship by this time and was living upriver in St. Helens with his father and his brother Willie. New Year's Eve was cold and the snow was very deep, so the Popes decided not to attend a party at a neighboring farm. Instead they fired off a cannon to celebrate the arrival of the new year, 1857. Pope copied the lyrics from a popular song into the last page of his 1856 diary. It was called "Good News from Home."

Good news from home—good news for me,
Has come across the deep blue sea,
From friends that I have left in tears—
From friends that I've not seen for years,
And since we parted long ago,
My life has been a scene of woe,
But now a joyful hour has come,
For I have heard good news from home.

Pope did not reflect much on his time sailing on *Desdemona* or the friends he had made. He noted when the ship passed by St. Helens and marked the anniversary of having been discharged from the ship, but his attentions had turned toward land-based issues such as helping neighbors round up lost cattle.

Captain Francis Williams had made good time from San Francisco until *Desdemona* hit a storm off the Oregon coast on December 31. The routine trip then turned dramatic. According to his account, the ship was damaged on New Year's Eve Day, "struck by a sudden squall, carrying away the jibboom, top gallant sails and topsails."

There were two routes into the Columbia River, and both the north and south channels required navigation around hazardous sandy spits and islands. Captain Williams reported that "having thus become crippled with the bar being dead under our lee," he was "determined to run the barque in by the north channel." He also claimed the lower buoy marker was missing, which would have made it more difficult to navigate the channel. Buoys in the 1850s contained bells that rang as the currents knocked into them. A 1,600-pound bell was also installed at Cape Disappointment for ships to hear when the weather was foggy.

The Columbia River Bar has destroyed countless vessels and taken many lives over the years. Tide and wind conditions had to be timed just right to make the crossing, and a pilot had to be available. Ships regularly had to wait several days outside of the river with no shelter from the unpredictable winds and large swells before making the crossing.

Captain Williams decided to guide *Desdemona* over the bar himself at high tide early on New Year's Day, 1857, without a pilot. It is not clear whether the captain signaled for a pilot or whether he had to take the ship in because there had been too much damage to properly control *Desdemona* in the rough swells offshore. He reported that "no pilot was in sight."[2]

The ship headed into the river, looking for the north channel. *Desdemona* sailed successfully past one of the biggest dangers, Clatsop Spit, which looks like a strong arm of sand sticking out from the south side of the river with a clenched fist at its end. The ship began making her way into the river. Without seeing the lower buoy, she struck a big sandbar in the middle of the river and was grounded. In the words of the captain, the ill-fated bark "got ashore on the middle sands abreadst of Chenook Point it being then high top water."

The hilly spot known as Chinook Point in what is now Washington State is where Captain Robert Gray anchored his ship *Columbia Rediviva* in 1792. She was the first American ship known to have entered the Columbia River. He met and traded with the local Chinook tribe living there. Chinook Point is also recognized as the spot where the Lewis and Clark Corps of Discovery camped when they first reached the Pacific Ocean after their journey west in 1805.[3]

The Middle Sands, as it was known then, is a shifting sandbar just below the surface of the water. Modern nautical guidelines say it stretches southeast for eight miles, starting just inside the Columbia River. Some parts of the sandbar are visible above the water during low tide.

Everyone on board *Desdemona* was safe after the initial grounding. The ship remained intact for all of New Year's Day and overnight, but was not able to refloat during high tide the next morning on January 2. A tug called *Joe Lane* tried unsuccessfully to pull the ship free. Interestingly, the tug was named for Joseph Lane, the first governor of the Oregon Territory, who had replaced Oregon Country governor and former owner of *Desdemona*, George Abernethy.

The ship began to leak. The stress of the waves and the constant pressure of the sand caused her to bilge, meaning the bottom part of the hull cracked open. *Desdemona* was doomed.

Captain Williams quickly rowed to Astoria and hired ten men to salvage as much of the ship's contents as they could before it was too late. The workers gathered the loads on the deck and began transporting the lighter cargo in smaller boats to shore. Some of the cargo was washed off the deck in rough swells, but many smaller items were saved.

A young man named George Cartland from St. Helens was helping with the salvage operation. His small dinghy was overcome by a wave, dumping him and several others into the surging, cold water. The others were able to pull themselves to safety, but George unfortunately drowned.

Seth Pope may have known George, since they both lived in St. Helens. In his diary, Pope wrote "Cartland's son drowned by sinking of scow. Our goods all gone, about $500. Vessel total loss." Nathaniel Cartland, George's father, was one of the first postmasters in St. Helens. Pope had learned about the wreck from the steamboat *Multnomah*, affectionately known as "Mult." The steamboat carried the mail and news back and forth along the Columbia River between Portland and Astoria.[4]

Among the survivors was nineteen-year-old Scotland native William Lewis, who had moved to Oregon in 1856. When he died in 1902, the wreck of *Desdemona* stood out in his obituary as a major event in his life. He went on to have a long career as a marine engineer and lived to be one of "the oldest men on the Columbia and Willamette River Runs."

Another inbound ship, the steamer *Columbia*, approached the mouth of the river one week after the wreck, on the evening of Friday, January 9, during a strong ebb tide. In his travelogue with the header "Letter from Oregon" published in the *Daily Alta California*, T. R. Anthony, Esq., was in awe of the passage across the bar: "Having heard and read much of the Columbia bar, I thought I was fully posted up with regard to its appearance, but I was mistaken, the half not been told me, neither did the description of it which I had read convey even a faint idea of what I then beheld for the first time." Anthony went on to detail what he witnessed: "Within about four miles of Astoria, we discovered a vessel close inland on our left, or starboard quarter. We run as close to her as it was safe to do, and found she was high and dry on what is called the 'Middle Sands' or 'Clatsop Point.' It proved to be the barque Desdemona, bound from San Francisco to Portland, with a cargo valued at some $35,000, which, together with the vessel, will be a total loss."

T. R. Anthony and the steamer *Columbia* made it safely across the bar, but ended up staying in Astoria into the weekend. Upriver, the water was reportedly frozen over. *Columbia*, which also carried mail to the territory, had to turn back to Astoria after encountering large fields of floating ice. She arrived back in San Francisco on January 14, bringing news of the wreck and the ice. "She brings no papers from Oregon, the Columbia river being frozen over. The Columbia was unable to ascend the river higher than Woody Island," the *Daily Alta California* reported.

Anthony went on to detail his adventure once river traffic reopened, claiming their ship was itself nearly wrecked farther upriver when she struck a rock. He took another ship when *Columbia* headed back to San Francisco. The wreck of *Desdemona* must have been both a curiosity and a sobering warning of danger for many passing ships.

In a letter dated January 13, nearly two weeks after the wreck, the captain of *Desdemona* made an odd statement, perhaps referring to the public recovering what remained of the ship and her cargo. "Clatsop Sea Pirates, by the way, are having a good time," he said. If he was referring to the Clatsop Indians, only about one hundred members of the tribe were left by the 1850 census. They had been stripped of their land despite an 1851 treaty with the US government and had suffered devastating losses from European diseases. The Donation Land Claim Act was giving away 320 acres to single white male settlers, 640 acres to married couples, as a way of increasing American settlement of the area in case the British tried to claim the region.

A salvage contract was given to Moses Rogers for $215, and he removed whatever was left of value from the wreck of *Desdemona*. The remaining hull was visible for many years. It was a landmark and a warning marker to direct other ships away from the big sandbar in the middle of the river. Navigational maps began to call the sandbar Desdemona Sands instead of the Middle Sands, as it had been known previously.

A Supreme Court case between the states of Oregon and Washington just after the turn of the twentieth century settled disputed ownership of the sandy islands near the mouth of the Columbia River, including Desdemona Sands. Several ship captains who were longtime residents of Astoria mentioned the wreck when they were called upon to testify about their experiences with the shipping channels and shifting sands in 1905.

When asked if there was ever a time when "ocean going vessels in coming from the ocean into Astoria, pursued a course north of Desdemona Sands," Captain John W. Welch said, "I have seen it from where we lived at home there. We could see right out across, and I have seen them come in that way, and when the *Desdemona* came in, she started that way, but she got too far in towards the shore, and she got aground on the point of the sandbar there, and that was what caused the name of that. We couldn't see her from home, couldn't see her from our house at all."

Captain P. E. Ferchen described himself as a part-time seaman and boat-keeper, "a man that when all the pilots had gone away he would take charge of the boats." He had a strong memory of the wreck and the sands to share during his testimony. "I beg your pardon," he said. "I

Desdemona Sands Lighthouse. **Courtesy of the US Lighthouse Society**

want to tell you, speaking about the Desdemona Sands, it was the year I came here or the year after that the *Desdemona* was wrecked on that sand, and I myself helped to take the crew off."

The wreck of *Desdemona* left a lasting impact on the area. After the Point Adams Lighthouse was decommissioned in 1899, a lighthouse was built on Desdemona Sands in 1901. Point Adams is on the southern side of the mouth of the Columbia River. That point of land kept the American name Robert Gray attached to it, unlike Cape Hancock on the north side, which retained the British name Cape Disappointment. Desdemona Sands Lighthouse stood on a wooden platform surrounded by wood pilings. The light guided ships away from suffering the fate of the bark *Desdemona* until the mid-1960s, when it was replaced by a lighted buoy. The foundations of the lighthouse pilings can still be seen today with remote imaging.

The last remains of the ship disappeared long ago, either buried under the sands as they shifted or washed away by a big storm. There may be nothing left in the original wreck location for maritime archaeologists to investigate today. Objects from the wreck, however, have found their way into local museum collections. They arrived many years, sometimes

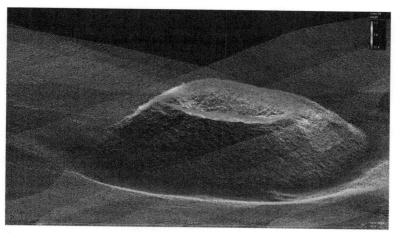

Ortho view of the Desdemona Sands Lighthouse foundation. **Courtesy of the US Army Corps of Engineers**

even generations, after the shipwreck. Some were collected as mementos, while others were pulled up accidentally by fishing nets. Tangible remains bring a sense of reality to the old stories. At the Columbia River Maritime Museum in Astoria, a handwritten index card catalogs the remaining remnants of the 104-foot-long *Desdemona*: a relic fragment, a copper draft pin, a timber fragment, a copper spike.

The shipwreck occurred during important formative years of the American Northwest. It was before the borders recognized today as the western states were in place, and it was less than five years before the Civil War consumed the United States. Missionaries, retired fur trappers, and other settlers were deciding which dreams and values of American culture they wanted to extend to the region. Even though only one person died related to the *Desdemona* wreck, a ship bringing the goods to help build those dreams had wrecked in a highly visible spot, with the remains left behind as if on display, which may have helped the three-masted bark pass into legend. The name Desdemona was later seen in local shops and on food packaging labels.

Many of the best-loved stories from history involve misfortune and tragedy. The wrecked bark shared a name associated with such tales. The passionate Desdemona of William Shakespeare's *Othello* was murdered by her enraged husband after he had been deceived into believing she committed adultery. The name Desdemona itself comes from a Greek term meaning "unfortunate" or "ill-fated."

Label for Desdemona brand canned salmon. **Courtesy of the Columbia River Maritime Museum, Astoria**

Desdemona Club on Marine Drive in Astoria, 2019. **Photographer Jennifer Kozik**

In Astoria, the wistful name is still remembered today. A seaward glance during a drive across the sage-green steel bridge connecting Oregon and Washington reveals Desdemona Sands at low tide, still stretching out along the middle of the river. Songs and poetry have been written about the sands. A bar at the east end of town, the Desdemona Club, is emblazoned with a bright pink neon sign. Inside is a painting of the lost bark in an oval frame, immortalized for local bar patrons above the wooden shufflepuck table.

Jennifer Kozik

GREAT REPUBLIC

LEISURELY KNOCKED TO PIECES, 1879

At midnight, a pilot boat pulled up alongside a large paddle-wheel steamer just west of Clatsop Spit outside the mouth of the Columbia River. At 4,000 tons and 350 feet long, *Great Republic* was one of the largest commercial vessels ever built in the United States. The fifty-foot-wide ship was propelled by two enormous side paddle wheels, each measuring forty feet in diameter.

The bar pilot, trained to navigate commercial and passenger vessels through the hazardous river mouth, climbed aboard. After making his way to the pilothouse, bar pilot Thomas Doig and Captain James Carroll discussed the fortunate weather. Light winds and flat seas were expected through the morning hours of April 19, 1879. Both captains agreed they should cross the bar into the Columbia River before dawn. They knew the Columbia River Bar to be a dangerous system of sand and sediment that collects at the mouth of the mightiest river on the Pacific Coast. The relatively narrow pass between the rocky outcrop of Cape Disappointment to the north and the Clatsop Spit to the south forces a tremendous amount of water into the ocean at a high rate of speed. This rapid outflow of water sometimes pushes against ocean swells, building tall waves, particularly at ebb tide. The weather that night was perfectly calm.

The steamer, which had slowed to receive the pilot boat, resumed cruising at a moderate speed. *Great Republic* headed north past Clatsop Spit and then turned northeast into the river. Pilot Doig was concerned the ship might not clear the shallow sands of Clatsop Spit and continued to steam northeast toward Sand Island. Captain Carroll realized the ship was getting too close to the island, and grew even more nervous as the ship neared the small atoll. Taking back control of his ship from the pilot, he ordered the helmsman, "Port your helm," but it was too late.

Great Republic was built in 1866 at the Henry Steers shipyard in Greenpoint, New York. She was one of four large steamships commissioned just after the Civil War to run mail, cargo, and passengers to the western Pacific. The Pacific Mail Steamship Company had been making runs between New York and San Francisco since 1848. At that time, passengers and cargo could travel around the South American Cape Horn from New York. Or, with the expansion of the railroads, travelers could take a ship to Panama, cross Panama by train, and then proceed

Great Republic *under construction; photograph with hand-painted flags.*

from Panama to San Francisco on another steamer. The company made a significant profit on the route because a huge flood of passengers was heading west for the California gold rush. The US government also provided substantial subsidies for transporting the mail. In 1865 the company decided to use a similar business model, purchasing four new steamers to carry mail, cargo, and passengers from China and Japan.

The ship was outfitted with a large walking beam engine that propelled the two paddle wheels. The stresses and strains of a North Pacific crossing required this class of ships to be built solidly. The frames were constructed from white and live oaks, which were covered with yellow pine planks. The frames were reinforced with a series of iron straps that fitted into the outboard face of the timbers. The iron straps measured five inches wide and nearly an inch thick. They were fitted diagonally across the frames, crisscrossing each other every four feet.

In August the following year, 1867, *Great Republic* steamed to its new home in San Francisco as the first ship of the new China Line. The *Daily Alta California* heralded the arrival of the new steamer.

> From stem to stern she is as perfect a steamer as can be produced in the world, and no successful steamer (the Great Eastern is simply a mammoth marine elephant, which regularly ruins a new set of owners with every trip) save her companion ship, China, now on her way here, now afloat, can in any manner compare with her. It would seem at first glance that she is too richly furnished and luxuriously fitted for the trade between this port and Japan and China; but when we take into consideration the fact that steamers of this line are to compete with the indifferently furnished, comparatively small, close and inconvenient steamers of the Peninsular and Oriental Steamship Co., running through the sickly regions of the equator, it will be readily seen that such advantages as they offer will not be thrown away on the public.

Despite the excitement created by the arrival of *Great Republic* on the Pacific Coast, the Pacific Mail Steamship Company was criticized for building wooden side-wheel ships when screw-propelled steel ships were proven to be faster and more reliable on the East Coast. The company did not see a need to switch to the newest American shipbuilding trend of metal construction. Side-wheel ships had been working perfectly well on their San Francisco to Panama routes. This decision would determine the relatively short life crossing the Pacific of *Great Republic* and her sister ships.

Great Republic and her three sister ships began passenger and mail runs to Yokohama, Japan, and Hong Kong in China. *Great Republic* began a six-week schedule in September 1867, meaning that the ship would steam to Asia and back, and then be ready to begin again within approximately forty-five days. By late 1868, steamers *China* and *Japan* were added. The fourth new steamer of the class, *America*, was sent around Africa, passing the Cape of Good Hope in October 1869. *America* headed to Singapore to pick up the first Chinese steerage passengers bound for the United States. The arrival of the new steamer in San Francisco gave the steamship company more flexibility to maintain a new monthly schedule and also provide time for additional maintenance of the fleet.

Great Republic could carry 250 cabin passengers and up to 1,500 additional passengers in the steerage compartment. Europeans and Americans occupied the well-furnished cabins and enjoyed good lighting and ventilation. The bathing areas were located just forward of the paddle wheels. The Chinese passengers remained in the steerage berthing area below, and while these accommodations were far less comfortable than the cabin arrangements, the area was reportedly kept clean and hospitable. Alexander von Graff Hübner traveled across the Pacific aboard the steamer China and described his visit to the steerage compartment with the captain.

> The Chinese quarter is on the lower deck. We have about 800 on board. They are all in their berths, smoking and talking and

enjoying the rare pleasure in their lives of being able to spend five weeks in complete idleness. In spite of the great number of men penned into comparatively small a space, the ventilation is so well managed that there is neither closeness nor bad smells. The captain inspects every hole and corner—literally everything—and everywhere we found the same extraordinary cleanliness. One small space is reserved for the opium eaters and smokers, and we saw these victims of a fatal habit, some eagerly inhaling their poison, others already feeling their effects.

Great Republic transported more than ten thousand immigrants from China to San Francisco, completing twenty-five voyages from 1867 to 1877. This equates to approximately 10 percent of the Chinese emigration into the United States at that time. Many of these passengers created Chinatowns, not just in San Francisco but across the West, including Portland and John Day, Oregon. A large number of Chinese immigrants also worked in the Astoria canneries. During the peak salmon season in 1880, the Clatsop County census noted 2,045 people of Chinese descent out of the total population of 7,055 people.

The Chinese Exclusion Act of 1882 suspended Chinese immigration for ten years and declared those who were already living here ineligible for citizenship. The act was renewed for another ten years, and then made permanent in 1902. The legislation caused a sharp decline in the Chinese population in the United States. It was not until 1943, when China and the United States were allies in World War II, that it was finally repealed.

The Pacific Mail Steamship Company faced its first competition in 1873 with the British China Transpacific Company, based in Hong Kong. This organization purchased new fast steamers from England, which set new speed records between Asia and San Francisco. Their rapid Pacific transits and luxurious accommodations forced the Pacific Mail Steamship Company to lower their cabin fares to $150 to Yokohama and $200 to Hong Kong. Despite their competitive cabin rates, China Transpacific Company steamers could not carry as many steerage passengers and were soon outperformed by the Pacific Mail ships.

Great Republic and the other wooden side-wheeled steamers faced their biggest threat from three new British steel-hulled, screw-driven steamers from the Occidental and Oriental Steamship Company. By 1878 Pacific Mail side-wheelers could barely keep up with them, so the company retired the ships in favor of newer, faster steamers with lower coal costs. *Great Republic* was sold to P. B. Cornwall, from San Francisco, and was placed on the coastal run up to Portland. Despite the huge coal cost to run the steamer, the ship could carry a large number of passengers, making the San Francisco to Portland run quite profitable. The ship carried a full load of passengers in each direction through late 1878 and early 1879. Some passengers rode the ship back and forth, essentially living on the ship, because the cost of a round-trip ticket was cheaper than finding housing ashore.

In the early morning hours of April 19, 1879, as the steamer *Great Republic* approached Sand Island near the mouth of the Columbia River, Captain Carroll tried to stop the disaster. "Port your helm," he had said to the pilot. Turning the bow of the ship to port, which is the left side of the ship, would have pushed her into shallow water. Some believe that the captain was trying to sail around the island. However, steering commands in the nineteenth century still reflected the old traditions of tiller steering. Before the use of a wheel to move a rudder, sailors used a horizontal beam, called a tiller, attached to the top of the rudder that was pushed in the opposite direction the helmsman desired the ship to travel. The command for the helmsman to port his rudder was actually to turn the ship to the right. Carroll was not trying to steer around Sand Island but instead he tried to turn southward back into the river and away from the shoal water. His order came too late, though, and the steamer slid onto the sandbar. The soft grounding did not immediately appear to signal the death of a ship with such a fine history.

The contact with the sandbar had been so slight that many of the passengers and crew did not realize that the ship was in trouble. Captain Carroll and the crew were confident the steamer would be refloated and they could head up the Columbia to their destination in Portland on the next high tide. Unfortunately, as the sea fell, the heavy weight of the machinery created stress on the hull. Leaks began trickling in through the bilges. The water injection pipes to the boilers broke off, which eliminated steam to the bilge pumps and allowed the water to encroach further.

The rising water of the next high tide was lower than the day before, and the ship stayed fast to the sandbar. Captain Carroll sent the 886 passengers ashore in Astoria so they could make other arrangements for the trip to Portland. The crew and a few determined passengers remained aboard. The ebbing tide continued to stress the hull of the ship and disable more of her machinery. In *Marine History of the Pacific Northwest*, Lewis and Dryden described the ship as being "leisurely knocked to pieces."

Finally, on the morning of April 21, Captain Carroll declared the ship lost and ordered everyone left on board to evacuate. All of the remaining passengers and most of the crew were rowed safely to

Great Republic *aground on Sand Island.* **Courtesy of the Columbia River Maritime Museum, Astoria**

Sand Island. The final launch departed the side of the ship at about 10:30 a.m. in slightly heavier seas and increasing westerly winds. The steering oar used by First Officer H. Lennon broke off. Witnesses reported seeing the small boat capsize, caught broadside by a breaker. Three of the crew swam to Sand Island, but eleven people died, including the first officer of *Great Republic*.[1]

The weather deteriorated rapidly as the barometer continued to drop. Captain Carroll described the ship's breakup.

> Heavy seas boarded the ship and carried away the staterooms on the starboard side, gutted the dining room, broke up the floor of the social hall, and carried away the piano. Several seas afterward boarded her forward and carried away the starboard guard, officer's room and steerage deck, also a number of horses. I remained on board until 5:00 p.m., when the pilot and myself lowered a lifeboat and came ashore.

The passengers were grateful to Captain Carroll for keeping them safe. They paid for an article in the local newspaper thanking Carroll as well as the captains and crews of the tugs that brought them ashore. The steamship *Little California* carried the majority of the passengers on to Portland. The horses on board were not so lucky. Only seven of the twenty-seven horses left behind managed to swim to Sand Island.

An inquiry was called to investigate who was at fault for the errors in judgment leading to the grounding. Captain Carroll had his license suspended for six months. He appealed the ruling, however, and got his license restored. Carroll continued to serve as master on other ships along the Pacific Coast, including many serving Alaska. Pilot Doig lost his license for a full year because of the wreck.

The ship was insured for $50,000 and the cargo for $25,000. The underwriters sold the wreck and cargo for $3,780 to a group who formed the Great Republic Wrecking Company. They removed what they could off the steamer before she broke apart completely. The weather and tides took several days to remove the superstructure and large portions of the bow. Within a few weeks, most of the hull had disappeared from view, leaving only the large walking beam engine and the paddle wheels. Army gunners at Fort Canby used the wreck for target practice, and the southern point of Sand Island became known as Republic Spit.

Eventually, the powerful river claimed the wreck and the steamer was lost from view. Sand on the bottom of the river swept over the wreckage as the years passed, unseen by the growing population on both sides of the river and by the multitude of ships passing near the old steamer. The late nineteenth and early twentieth centuries brought the construction of two jetties on the south and north edges of the river, jutting out into the Pacific. They were designed to control the unpredictable movement of sand in the area. The jetties slowed, but did not stop, the movement and changing shape of Sand Island. Republic Spit disappeared from the charts, and *Great Republic* passed into history.

In the fall of 1986, more than a century after the wreck, a fisherman snagged a new net on an obstruction just south of Sand Island. A local scuba diver freed the net from an old wooden shipwreck and recovered a small section of a ship timber. The wood section contained a treenail, which is much like a large wooden dowel, used to fasten wooden planks. Treenails (pronouced "trunnels") were used to join planks on older wooden ships. The timber was taken to the Columbia River Maritime Museum in Astoria for further analysis. The fisherman was well versed in local nautical history and believed the wreck could have been the Hudson's Bay Company brig *Isabella*, which was lost in the same vicinity in 1830. The maritime museum staff thought it was an interesting suggestion, but they were not entirely convinced. There were many wooden shipwrecks in the Graveyard of the Pacific. Only a few, however, were older wooden ships that sank near Sand Island, including *Great Republic*.

Isabella was an eighty-four-foot-long, English-built merchant brig used to carry cargo long distances. The Hudson's Bay Company purchased the sturdy ship in 1829 to service Fort Vancouver along the Columbia River. *Isabella* reached the hazardous river entrance in 1830 and struck the sandbar several times, tearing off her rudder. The captain ordered the crew to jettison some of the cargo in an attempt to lighten the ship enough to free the bar, but their efforts were in vain. That evening the captain and crew abandoned *Isabella* and headed up the Columbia River to Fort Vancouver in their small boats.

A rescue crew from the fort made it back to *Isabella* but found that the anchor chain had broken. The ship was aground and breaking apart near Sand Island. Rather than attempt to refloat the brig, the rescuers worked to salvage part of the cargo. They cut a rough square hole in the side of the vessel to access the cargo hold and the remaining un-jettisoned provisions. After loading up all they could save, the salvagers headed back to Fort Vancouver. Little else remains in the written record about what happened to the wreckage of *Isabella*. The American fur-trading post of Astoria nearby had been founded less than twenty years earlier in 1811.

The Columbia River Maritime Museum organized a group of local divers to investigate the old wooden shipwreck snagged by the net of the fisherman. Together they conducted over forty dives on the site and developed a rough sketch of the vessel remains. The data collected by the local divers caught the interest of the Submerged Cultural Resource Unit of the National Park Service (NPS).

NPS divers investigated the site in August 1987 and completed a mapping of the submerged structure. In addition to mapping the site by hand, the crew used the Sonic High Accuracy Ranging and Positioning System, known as SHARPS. The system uses a set of underwater sonic transducers to assist in drawing the site diagram.

Both the local dive team and the NPS divers faced challenging dive conditions. The strong currents of the river allow for only two twenty-minute dive windows during the slack tide periods. The water in the river is cold and murky, and maneuvering around the site could be dangerous. The area was filled with numerous obstructions, including an array of fishing nets and other debris.

The NPS divers mapped eighty feet of the wreck site. They noted five open ports that appeared to correlate with the attempted salvage of *Isabella*. Additionally, another roughly hewn square opening was located

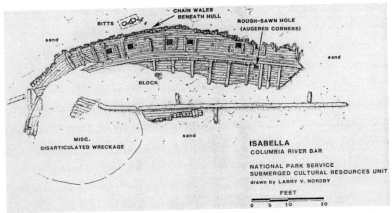

Site drawing of the wreckage initially believed to be the Hudson's Bay Company ship Isabella. *Courtesy of the National Park Service*

below the other five ports. This additional opening seemed to fit with the historical report of the square hole the rescue team cut in the side of *Isabella* to retrieve her cargo.

Given the presence of this roughly cut opening, and the lack of any evidence to counter the theory that the wreck site was *Isabella*, the NPS divers concluded that the wreck was the Hudson's Bay Company brig. The site was listed on the National Register of Historic Places as the final resting spot of *Isabella*.

Archaeological sites, particularly those listed on the National Register of Historic Places, are frequently monitored to see if humans have disturbed them or if they have been damaged by natural events. In 1994 the executive director of the Columbia River Maritime Museum, Jerry Ostermiller, conducted a monitoring survey of the wreck site. The dive team located the site and most of the features identified in the 1987 survey. However, they also found an additional twenty feet of hull structure and indications of large metal features. These discoveries ran counter to the identification of the site as the remains of *Isabella*.

The second monitoring dive took place in 1996. It was headed by James Delgado, who was the director of the Vancouver Maritime Museum in British Columbia at the time and had been a member of the NPS dive team in 1987. Members of the Underwater Archeological Society of British Columbia also participated in the dive. The dive team measured the total length of the wreckage and found it to be longer than eighty-four feet, the overall length of the brig *Isabella*. Diagonal iron straps, not likely found on a small brig, were also identified on the newly exposed section. Still, the presence of the roughly cut hole in the side continued to convince some archaeologists that the wreck must be *Isabella*.

The final dive on the site took place in 2004, by James Delgado. The wreckage was more exposed, and the underside of the structure was scoured clear. A second square-shaped opening was visible, as were the outboard edges of the roughly cut boxes. Both openings showed a lead lining similar to the lead lining of the open ports above them. The historical record did not indicate more than one opening cut into the hull of *Isabella* by the salvagers. The lead lining indicated that the holes were not the result of ad hoc actions conducted during an emergency, but rather that they were planned structural features. The dive team also recovered a section of wood that was determined to be southern yellow pine, indicating that the ship was constructed in America and not England.

The initial archaeological evidence from 1987 seemed to fit the theory that the wreck site was *Isabella*. The eighty-foot size of the exposed structure at that time, the lack of large metal features, and the apparent roughly hewn opening that matched historical statements all indicated the eighty-four-foot brig was the best choice. Site monitoring is a vital archaeological practice. In this case, the reexamination of the site provided valuable new information including an additional twenty feet of structure, forcing archaeologists to reassess their findings. The remains had to be from a ship that was at least one hundred feet long. For submerged maritime archaeological sites, the conditions are always changing. A site may be damaged, destroyed, or in this case, further revealed between site visits.

With *Isabella* disqualified, *Great Republic* took shape as a new candidate for the identity of the wreck site. The iron straps on the side of the

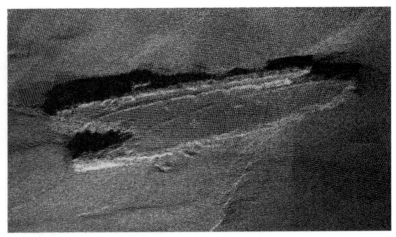

Multi-beam sonar of the wreckage. **Courtesy of the US Army Corps of Engineers**

hull match the type of structure used by steamers of that time. *Great Republic* was 350 feet long, which exceeds the length of hull exposed on the bottom. The hull of the steamer was made of white oak and yellow pine, which matches the type of material recovered from the site. Several other large metal objects recorded at the site, such as iron bollards, match what might be expected on *Great Republic*. The location of the site, at the south end of Sand Island, fits the description of Republic Spit. No other ships with these physical characteristics have been identified in the historical or archaeological databases.

Primary investigators Delgado and Ostermiller summarized the new findings. They stated that the Sand Island wreck best fits the paddle-wheel steamer *Great Republic*. This new interpretation is based on what they call a chain of circumstantial evidence, but without the "smoking gun" they thought they had with the earlier identification. "We were misled not because our assumptions were improper," they said, "but because our assumptions were simply based upon the best information we had at the time, and we could not see all of the evidence."[2]

This is how science works. All available data in the 1980s appeared to prove the old wooden shipwreck snagged by a fishing net was the brig *Isabella*. New observations, however, can bring long-held conclusions into question and lead to further study. Researchers in Astoria from the Maritime Archaeological Society continue to investigate the Sand Island wreck with hopes of making a positive identification. Research vessels monitoring the Columbia River navigational channel visit the wreck site frequently. The US Army Corps of Engineers also routinely scans the exposed surfaces of the wreck site using multi-beam sonar, which provides site monitoring data about the state of the wreck.

A momentary error in judgment pushed *Great Republic* onto a sandbar to be gently demolished by the tides and currents of the Columbia River, while a likely misidentification delayed the rediscovery of her remains for many years. The search for a definitive identification of the suspected wreck site continues. *Great Republic* has an important legacy too. The ship that had carried thousands of Chinese immigrants to new lives across the Pacific, and helped to shape the late nineteenth-century US immigration story, may one day be able to join the National Register of Historic Places.

Christopher Dewey

EMILY REED

A DISASTROUS FOGGY VALENTINE'S DAY, 1908

*E*mily G. Reed was built in the waning years of the great sailing ships. Wind power was giving way to coal-driven steam engines. The days of ships powered by billowing, wind-filled white sails were coming to an end with the rise of noisy engines coughing out black smoke through funnels while turning a screw propeller below the surface of the water.

Emily Reed was a wooden-hulled sailing ship known as a downeaster. This type of large sailing cargo ship was built in Maine during the last three decades of the nineteenth century. They were originally built to sail downwind and east for trade between Maine and Boston. Not to be confused with the much smaller modern sailboat and fishing craft on the northeast coast known as downeasters today, *Emily Reed* was 215 feet long and over 40 feet wide at the beam, with a 24-foot hold depth. The ship, built in 1880 in Waldoboro, Maine, by A. R. Reed & Co, was rated to carry 1,467 net tons and was named for a member of the Reed family. They also built ships named *Alice Reed, Isaac Reed, Annie Reed,* and *Willie Reed* over the course of a decade. The vessel was ideal for international shipping: fast and versatile, with three masts and a sleek hull. *Emily Reed* was purchased by Yates and Porterfield of New

Emily Reed *at port, date unknown.* **Courtesy of the Peabody Essex Museum, Salem**

York for trade on the high seas. She departed December 9, 1880, on her maiden voyage, sailing from New York to Calcutta with case oil.

The sailing ship had around six different captains over her lifetime and survived dramatic encounters with storms, dumped cargo, and accusations of abuse of the crew by officers. In 1888 she arrived in New York from Singapore with a damaged top mast. In 1891 she was damaged again, hobbling to Rio de Janeiro with a temporary rudder after a storm. The captain at the time, Sheldon, and his crew were able to steer the ship to port by "tackle over each quarter," which involves using ropes and blocks or pulleys mounted at the two far corners of the stern to control the position of a temporary rudder. After both of these incidents, the ship was repaired and put back into service. *Emily Reed* spent her last ten years in the Pacific, primarily carrying coal, sugar, and lumber. Her ports of call ranged from Sydney and Newcastle in Australia to Honolulu, San Francisco, Portland, and Seattle.

Strategically placed cities around the Pacific functioned as coaling stations for the steamship industry, which was by this time taking over ocean commerce. It was more economical to use sailing ships like *Emily*

Reed to transport the coal to these coaling stations, since they were considered to be a less efficient, aging fleet of outdated vessels. Steamships were newer and could travel faster, and they could maneuver into smaller secondary ports easier because their movements were less dependent on the winds and weather. The steam vessels did, however, burn through a lot of coal. The earliest oceangoing steam vessels also carried sails as a backup before coaling stations were readily available.

In early 1901, en route between Sydney and Honolulu, a southern Pacific storm caused *Emily Reed* to lose her sails, topmasts, and yardarms. The crew was able to patch together sufficient replacement sails to make it back to Sydney for repairs. The ship finally arrived in Honolulu on July 4 of that year with her load of coal. The Hawaiian Islands had been annexed by the United States just three years earlier in July 1898 despite the protests of native Hawaiians.

The *Pacific Commercial Advertiser*, a daily newspaper published in Honolulu, marked the arrival: "The Reed is a splendid vessel and came into port looking spick and span as a new ship. In fact, most of her gear is new and she has a new main lower-mast, the latter being of steel." The paper described what Independence Day in 1901 was like for sailors visiting the island: "A few firecrackers were exploded, but those who had been ashore all day seemed to much prefer ending the day with music. The songs of sailors gathered on the forecastle heads, loud, vibrating, strong, sea songs of men who go down to the sea in ships, added to the general tone of and appreciation of the day of recreation which comes only too seldom to the men who slave before the mast."

It was the common sailors who slept in the forecastle, which is the enclosure above or below the main deck at the bow of the ship, known as "before the mast." The nautical phrase was brought to popular attention through such nineteenth-century literature as *Two Years Before the Mast* by Richard Henry Dana Jr. and *Moby Dick* by Herman Melville. "No, when I go to sea," the lead character Ishmael in *Moby Dick* said, "I go as a simple sailor, right before the mast, plumb down into the forecastle, aloft there to the royal mast-head." A berth at the front of the ship, where a vessel first hits the dip of a wave, could be much rougher than sleeping aft. The officers and cabin boy slept in the enclosure at the stern of the ship near the wheelhouse.

Emily Reed was loaded with sugar in Hawaii and had prepared to leave when the captain and two mates were arrested for cruelty to members of the crew while at sea. The arrests took place during a time in the early twentieth century when maritime workers were joining together to form larger industrial unions. From dock workers to sailors, there was a concerted effort along the West Coast and at other ports in the Pacific to fight for better working conditions. The captain and first officer of *Emily Reed* were allowed to proceed to San Francisco, with a request that they later return to Hawaii to settle the charges.

The next tempest facing *Emily Reed* began on Christmas Eve 1905, when she was headed to Sydney from Chemainus, British Columbia, loaded with lumber. The ship sailed into a typhoon, and the seas surrounding her swelled like mountains. The canvas sails were reduced as much as possible. The ship became completely unmanageable, and for a time their situation was critical. According to the ship's officers, gigantic seas rose like great walls and descended with terrific violence on the decks, swamping every portion of the vessel, which labored and strained in the swells.

Three and a half feet of water had found its way into the hold. The anxiety level of the crew must have been intense. The pumps were put into operation, with everyone working unceasingly. Two days later on Boxing Day, after a consultation between the master and his officers, they decided to jettison the deck cargo as the only means to save the ship. An estimated 140,000 to 170,000 board feet of lumber was thrown overboard. It was not until December 30 that the tempest finally moderated. After surviving the Christmas storm, there was enough spar and sail to make it back to Sydney. Once there, the master at the time, Captain Reed, was able to convince the owners in San Francisco that the ship was once again worth saving and she was repaired.

For her next brush with disaster, *Emily Reed* grounded on Desdemona Sands near the mouth of the Columbia River on May 13, 1907.

The local *Morning Astorian* reported that "she is high and dry and it will take some time to kedge her off." "Kedging" is a nautical term used to describe setting a small anchor, a kedge, away from the ship and then pulling the ship to the anchor. It is a way to move vessels short distances when trying to get off a shoal or move against strong currents. By the following day, the ship had slowly eased into deeper waters. The twenty-six-year-old vessel survived this journey, and continued on her way. The ship would not be so lucky the next time she headed for Portland.

Six months later, on November 3, 1907, *Emily Reed* departed the port of Newcastle, Australia, on what would be her final journey. Bound for Portland, Oregon, she had a new captain, William Kessel of San Francisco, and a load of coal. Kessel's wife and fifteen other crew members were on board. The sailing ship had made previous trips between Australia and the West Coast in fifty-four days. Sixty days went by, then ninety days. No one heard from *Emily Reed*. She was so long overdue that the Alaska Fishermen's Packing Association, which held her charter, decided the ship must have been lost at sea. They made arrangements to charter another ship, *Henry Villard*, to take her place. The replacement charter was set in place on February 5, 1908.

More than a week later, *Emily Reed* finally approached the Oregon coast. The ship had been out of contact for 103 days. Captain Kessel later told the *Daily Oregon Journal* the weather had been unfavorable since they left Australia. "The vessel encountered headwinds for most of the passage and fought several fearful blows," he said. Despite the arduous passage, the ship had withstood the strain of the journey.

Emily Reed had survived several terrible storms and a recent grounding on Desdemona Sands. As she undertook this fateful trip, the ship was encumbered with 2,110 tons of coal when usually she carried closer to 1,500 tons of cargo. Overloaded, battered, and with a crew who must have been weary after the arduous weather during the 103-day journey from New Castle, the ship approached the coast.

The captain tried to spot the shore. He was hoping to get a visual fix on the Tillamook Rock Lighthouse in order to confirm the accuracy of his navigation after having been so long at sea. There was dense fog in the earliest hours of Valentine's Day 1908 when *Emily Reed* sailed along the rugged and sparsely populated coast. According to his calculations, Captain Kessel believed he was well offshore near Tillamook Head. Tillamook Head is the rocky headland rising over one thousand feet above the sea between the towns of Seaside and Cannon Beach, where Ecola State Park is today. They were actually farther south, near the entrance of the Nehalem River.

It was after 1:30 a.m. on Friday, February 14. Twenty-two-year-old Spanish seaman Vicente Sanchez was on deck getting ready to take his shift on the 2:00 a.m. watch. He had just finished helping to adjust the square sails perpendicular to the centerline of the ship, known as "squaring a yard." Suddenly they could hear the sound of breakers. The ship was much too close to the shore.[1]

First mate Fred Zube was on deck in the forward part of the ship. He was preparing to call all hands on deck when the ship struck the sand. With 2,110 tons of coal in her hold, the strain was more than the wooden structure could withstand. The ship began to break up almost immediately.[2]

Near the bow where Zube was standing, the part of the ship that struck the sand first, the entire forward section was breaking off from the rest of the ship and beginning to tip sideways. Three members of the crew who slept "before the mast"—Ole Sordveit, the cook from Norway, and seamen Ewald Abildstedt and Arthur Jahunke, both from Germany—stumbled out of their berths in the forecastle "with scarcely any clothing on their backs." Rigging and other debris was falling everywhere, and large swells threatened to knock them overboard. As the bow broke off, the aft section of the ship turned sideways, parallel to the shore.

At the aft end of the ship, the captain, who was only wearing nightclothes and a thin robe, grasped the wheelhouse door, the arms of his wife clasped tightly around his neck. Second mate Charles Thompson and three seamen—Sanchez, Lawrence Sullivan, and Herman Bartels—raced toward the back of the ship. "We hurried aft," Sanchez said, "and as she broke up the surf broke over us." A breaker knocked the wheel-house door off. Seaman Sullivan was able to grab on to the captain and his wife before they were washed overboard, and helped them back to the wheelhouse.

They clung close together, holding on for their lives. Several of the men tied themselves to the roof of the wheelhouse. Some later accounts said the captain made his wife stay below during the ordeal. Sanchez remembered differently and thought she was a hero for trying to help the cabin boy, Ernest Hirschfeld, who was trying to reach them. He heard her say "Give me your hand, Ernest, I'll save you. Can't you see my hand, boy, here, here." A loose swinging boom knocked Ernest into the sea unfortunately, and she was unable to save him.

Zube, the cook, and the other two seamen on the careening bow knew they could not reach the others, so they jumped into the only forward lifeboat. The other lifeboat had been smashed by the surging breaking waves. The bow of *Emily Reed* was quickly breaking away from the rest of the ship. Their lifeboat was knocked free from the ship by a big wave, damaged but upright.

In the early morning hours before dawn, the captain lost sight of the lifeboat in the black turgid water, swirling with wreckage of the rigging, masts, and sails. The six of them, holding on to the wheelhouse at the stern of the ship, appeared to be the only survivors. The four men in the lifeboat, along with the seven other members of his crew, were gone, swept away into the darkness and dense fog.

With the first morning light, one of the crew members prepared himself to swim to shore for help. Seaman Sullivan tied a line to him-self and jumped from the aft section of the ship into the sea. The tide was at low ebb, and he discovered the water was only waist deep. He was able to carry a line to shore and secure it there. The others followed, with the captain and seaman Sanchez assisting Mrs. Kessel. They all made it to shore safely.

Rockaway Beach has seven miles of shoreline, and the area was sparsely inhabited in the early twentieth century. The *Oregon Daily Journal* reported that they first walked north toward the mouth of the

Nehalem River three miles away, "but seeing no sign of habitation they retracted their steps and, forced to high ground they struggled along over logs and driftwood against a driving rain until noon, when they finally reached the home of E. J. Hadley at Oceanlake Park, completely exhausted from their terrible experience." Oceanlake Park is today known as Spring Lake. It is roughly adjacent to the area of Twin Rocks, which poke up out of the water just offshore. The shivering survivors had spent half the day trying to find shelter. Three of them had no shoes or socks. They were all bruised from their harrowing ordeal, battered by breakers and floating wreckage.

They were taken to Bay City, farther south inside Tillamook Bay. Sullivan and Sanchez were praised for their heroic work during the ordeal. Captain Kessel reported the wreck and the deaths of the rest of his crew. "A heavy sea was on and a strong tide was running. When she hit the beach her back broke and the forward end took a list to port," he was quoted by the *Morning Astorian* as saying. "An effort was made to launch a lifeboat, but as soon as it hit the water it swamped and the four occupants were drowned before the eyes of those who were left on board. The men forward were swept from the deck by waves. The first mate was washed overboard and drowned while trying to direct the movements of the men forward." Eleven men were reported lost from the crew of seventeen: the first mate, the cook, the carpenter Peter Westerlund of Finland, seven seamen, and the cabin boy from Germany, Ernest Hirschfeld.

The captain was wrong about the fate of his first mate and the occupants of the lifeboat, however. Farther north, a different drama was playing out. The account of Zube, the first mate, was later released by the Associated Press and printed in newspapers all along the West Coast. "We jumped into the remaining lifeboat and cut at the lashings," he recounted. "A big wave broke over the wreck and carried us clear. A second wave carried away part of the galley deck roof, and it was hard work clearing the boat of the wreckage."

Zube suffered a broken arm from the falling debris. They tried unsuccessfully to get back to the wreck in the darkness, and knew their lifeboat would not be able to make it to shore safely in the swells. Eventually, "believing all hands, save ourselves, were lost, we got up sail and stood out to sea. As I knew the coast to be a desolate one, I thought it best to keep the boat well out, hoping to fall into the path of steamships. With this idea I set the course northbound."

The lifeboat was damaged and taking on water. There was only one oar, which was also partially damaged, and nothing to use for bailing out the water. Eventually they managed to carve off a piece of the watertight compartment on the lifeboat to use as a scoop. They continued north, taking turns bailing out the water, all the while hoping to find another ship. The hours dragged on, all through the day and night from Friday into Saturday.

"The second night out we saw lights ashore, but it was too dark for us to venture in," Zube continued. "There was neither food nor water, and we suffered terribly from thirst. Toward the evening the cook declared he could not stand it any longer and took a drink of sea water. He soon became delirious and lay down in the pool of water in the bottom of the boat. About 2 o'clock Sunday morning we saw a big steamer. She stopped near us, and we all believed we should be saved at once."

They encouraged the Norwegian cook to rouse himself. "He got on his feet and seemed rational as he watched the steamer. Just then the vessel got underway again and left us. Then the cook gave up the fight. He lay down to die. Half an hour later we found his body cold; his heart had stopped beating."

Around 11:00 p.m. on the night of February 16, almost three days after the wreck of *Emily Reed*, the crew of a small sloop at anchor in Neah Bay heard weak cries in the darkness coming from a steel lifeboat. "The three survivors were in a pitiable condition," the AP article reported. "Their tongues were swollen from thirst so at first they could scarcely articulate." The crew of the sloop *Teckla* helped the men aboard, offering them food and water. It was their first drink of water since before 1:30 a.m. early Friday morning.

First officer Zube and seamen Ewald Abildstedt and Arthur Jahunke were saved. They had survived a trip in a small, open boat with one sail and one broken oar, without water, provisions, rest, or adequate clothing. Their lifeboat had sailed all the way to the northern tip of Washington State. The three crewmen were taken to see a doctor in Neah Bay, and the broken arm of the first mate was set.

The direct route from Nehalem Bay to Tatoosh Island in Neah Bay is about 195 miles. The lifeboat, which was wandering at the mercy of wind and current, likely traveled more than two hundred miles. Official weather records show that winds over those two days were mostly out of the southeast and ranged from twelve to fifty-two miles per hour. These winds would have blown the frail craft far out to sea if not properly managed. There was also a strong current running north, especially strong along the Washington coast. Heavy swells would have made it suicidal to attempt to reach the shore with their small craft. The boat would have been swamped in the breakers and all would have surely drowned. It is miraculous that the little boat made the journey all the way up to Neah Bay.

The breakers continued pounding the wreckage of *Emily Reed* down on the Oregon coast. After the bow first struck the shore and began to list, the vessel was severed amidships at the mainmast. The stern swung broadside to the relentless surf, as evidenced by photos taken after the wreck. The rolling action contributed to the settling of the aft section of the ship into the deep sand, leaving that portion standing upright. One local resident, Elmer D. Allen, recalled the aftermath of the wreck years later in the *Tillamook Herald*: "She lay fast in the sand, broken in two with a pile of coal two stories high; masts, spars and sails toppled and her cargo of coal dumped to the center holding firmly the fore and aft. The beach was strewn with wreckage and coal."

The wave action, while strong and relentless enough to separate the forward sections, did not overwhelm the entire aft deck. The wheelhouse on the stern where the survivors were positioned remained relatively intact, with its shoreward railing still standing. Local newspapers reported the ship and her 2,110 tons of coal a total loss. Salvage rights to the wreckage on the beach were sold for $55 to a general merchandiser named John Nelson.

Pieces of copper and wood from the ship were picked up by local residents and tourists, along with coal from the broken cargo hold. It is a natural human tendency to pick up things found on the beach, either as useful items or as interesting mementos. Rummaging among cargo and material from shipwrecks strewn on beaches has probably been a tradition in coastal communities around the world for as long as there have been shipwrecks. Governments, ship owners, and other stakeholders have long tried to stop scavenging by locals, with little success. It is especially difficult to protect wreckage when it is spread over a large area.

Wreckage from *Emily Reed* was found as far away as the Columbia River, more than forty miles north of the wreck site. Of the remaining missing sailors, most were never found. The body of seaman Arthur Dixon, who had been on lookout duty at the time of the wreck, washed ashore days later. On February 18, Walter Frey from the Fort Canby lifesaving crew told the *Morning Astorian* the rudder from an *Emily Reed* lifeboat was found at Sand Island. A cylinder record for a phonograph was found in a box labeled *Emily Reed* that same week. The stern

Wreckage of Emily Reed *on the beach with Don Best's mother before the bow became buried in the sand.* **Courtesy of Don Best**

section likely moved several miles north and broke up, settling in multiple areas. Large pieces of wreckage have been reported near Manhattan Beach and in a creek close to Nehalem Bay.

The bow settled on its side and eventually sunk in the sand on Rockaway Beach. It was still pointing inward, toward shore, where the ship struck. The bow wreckage disappeared sometime in the 1950s or early 1960s. Walking along the beach south of the Nehalem River at low tide today, a person could step right over what remains of *Emily Reed* and never know it.

In the winter of 2008, one hundred years after the wreck of *Emily Reed*, wave actions from a big storm briefly scraped away the sand covering a section of the wreck. Her frames were once again visible. *Emily Reed* was built with New England pine planking over Georgia oak frames and had copper sheathing later added below the waterline to deter ship worms and other marine growth. Most of the pine planking and copper were salvaged or scavenged long ago. Planks taken from the wreckage are still covered in green corroded copper nails, which were used to fasten the copper sheathing to the outer hull. Iron bolts, driven

The Best family with Emily Reed *wreckage. Planking was still attached.* **Courtesy of Don Best**

Wreckage of Emily Reed *when it emerged in 2010.* **Courtesy of the photographer, Don Best**

through the frames to hold the ship together, remain on the frames. Washers or rings were put over the end of the bolts and the bolts were then crimped or flattened over the washers. The frames have occasionally been visible in the winter since 2008, showing themselves in 2010 and again in 2017. The construction details are still evident on the remaining wreckage.

It can be difficult to educate the public about not removing any wood or artifacts from a shipwreck. A person might think they are helping by dragging the wood off the beach to keep it from being thrown on a bonfire or reclaimed by the sea. Proper conservation to remove the salt and water is an expensive and time-consuming undertaking, however. Oregon state archaeologist Dennis Griffin advocates for leaving objects at the mercy of the tides: "It is best to let them be reclaimed by the sea and sand from future storms. Such wreck sites are usually better preserved buried offshore or beneath our beaches than being exposed to the elements."

There are laws protecting shipwrecks. The Abandoned Shipwreck Act of 1988 asserts US title to any abandoned shipwreck embedded in the submerged lands of a state. In Oregon, ORS 390.235 protects archaeological and historic material sites on public lands from excavations. And it prohibits the removal of any material from a site without a permit. "Protection under state and federal law in no way ensures a site's protection. As with other types of archaeological sites, many people remain unaware of the significance of shipwrecks, the knowledge of laws protecting such sites, and the harm that could result from their inquisitiveness," Dr. Griffin explained in the *Journal of Northwest Anthropology*.

No formal site report has been made of the known *Emily Reed* wreckage, which appears to measure over one hundred feet. Students at the University of Washington ran a pollen analysis on coal from the beach to verify its Australian origin. Pieces of coal from the wreck can be found at the Tillamook Pioneer Museum, Garibaldi Museum, and other institutions.

There may be several other pieces of the wreck left for maritime archaeologists to document. Local resident Don Best grew up near the wreck. "My dad said there are three pieces down by the creek on the south side," Best said. "Then there is a piece I believe is from the same ship because it is the same construction up by the Nehalem Jetty."[3]

Whenever the known beach wreckage makes an appearance, researchers from the Maritime Archaeological Society try to visit the site. The team takes measurements and looks for notable details in the construction methods and materials to photograph. This data can later

MAS volunteers measuring wreckage of Emily Reed *on the beach in 2017.* **Courtesy of the Maritime Archaeological Society**

MAS volunteers looking for diagnostic details to compare with other possible wreckage in the future. **Courtesy of the Maritime Archaeological Society**

be used to compare with other possible wreckage sites to determine their potential connection with *Emily Reed*. It is important to educate beachgoers about the site too. Sharing the history of the ship and the importance of recording shipwrecks will help preserve an interest in saving maritime heritage for future generations to rediscover when the sands reveal the wreck again.

Theodore "Tod" Lundy

GLENESSLIN

ICONIC SAILING SHIP VS. NEAHKAHNIE MOUNTAIN, 1913

Few hikers venture very far out onto the rocks north of Manzanita around the base of Neahkahnie Mountain. A handful of old crab cages and an occasional piece of plastic with Japanese text, perhaps tsunami debris from the 2011 earthquake in Japan, are left to bleach in the sun along with driftwood at the highest storm tide line. Rebar and chunks of concrete from the construction of Highway 101, along with beer cans tossed from the cliff at the scenic viewpoint high above, can be found here too. Hardy surfers have their own ways to reach the area. They fearlessly scramble down the rocks and ease into the cold water with their boards in search of good waves.

Walking northward from the beach, the sand turns to cobbles and then to large round boulders where the headland juts out into the sea. Eventually, pieces of rusted iron come into view, twisted and tumbled among the big rocks. It was here in October 1913 that a large ship in full sail crashed into the base of Neahkahnie Mountain. Locals and visitors took many photographs of the ruined vessel that autumn. They are some of the most enduring and iconic historical Pacific Northwest shipwreck images.

The ship was the three-masted British schooner *Glenesslin*. She had a long life prior to her encounter with the mountain. The hardy, fully rigged iron vessel was built in Liverpool in 1885 at the T. Royden & Sons shipyard. Registered at 260 feet long and a little over 39 feet wide, the ship had a hold that was more than 23 feet deep and a capacity of over 1,800 gross tons. Large cargo sailing vessels like *Glenesslin* were nicknamed windjammers. Iron hulls required less maintenance and took up less space, although their riveted hull joints did sometimes create lines of weak points that could split open under stress. Welded hulls did not become common until World War II.

Glenesslin crisscrossed the oceans, carrying cargo to and from Pacific Coast cities. In July of 1891 she arrived in San Pedro, Los Angeles, from Newcastle, New South Wales, with 2,700 tons of coal and then headed back to the United Kingdom with wheat in early October. The ship carried various goods around the world, whatever the contract required.

A serious fire in September 1894 nearly destroyed the ship. *Glenesslin* was moored near Watson Stores in Brooklyn, New York. Smelling smoke, the night watch boarded *Glenesslin* and opened a hatch cover. Smoke came billowing out from deep inside the ship. Her cargo hold held fifty thousand cases of volatile oil and another twenty-five thousand cases waited to be loaded nearby. Soon the entire inside of the metal ship was in flames, perhaps fueled by the oxygen added by the open hatch. Brooklyn fire crews tried to douse the flames and contain the fire. Everyone feared the cargo might explode, spreading destruction to the wharf and nearby vessels. The decision was made to scuttle the ship. It was the only way to stop the out-of-control inferno. Water filled the ship, dousing the flames and sinking *Glenesslin* at the dock. Newspapers at the time reported the vessel would be a total loss.

Captain Thomas Barlow Pritchard was master of *Glenesslin* for at least fifteen years. He spoke of the 1894 fire to the *San Francisco Call* a year later: "Unfortunately for all concerned, three days before we were to sail the ship took fire in the aft end underneath the cabin. In order to save the vessel, the fire brigade sank her. My wife and I had been away to Philadelphia to bid our friends goodbye, and when we returned to the Glenesslin she was eight feet underwater." The cost to repair the damage from the fire and sinking was $30,000.

Glenesslin was a well-built ship with high-quality furnishings. A journalist took a tour of the ship in 1898 for the *Eastern Province Herald* in Port Elizabeth, South Africa.

> The impressions left on his mind, however, were that the "Glenesslin" was one of the best and handsomest craft of its kind afloat; well found in every particular, and that the accommodation for the officers and crew left nothing that could be desired. The announcement of the steward that lunch was on the table brought us down to the Captain's private quarters, and we were not a little astonished to behold the sumptuousness of the apartments. A spacious private saloon, handsomely furnished, we were ushered into, from the paneling of which hung numerous handsome photographs, the most conspicuous being a fine bromide enlargement of the "Glenesslin" and life-sized bust portraits of the Captain and Mrs. Pritchard. Leading off from the saloon were the captain's sleeping cabins, bathroom and lavatory, all of which are fitted up with the latest improvements and in the best style.

The captain often traveled with his wife, Catherine, and their daughter, Kate. His wife unfortunately died in Antwerp, Belgium, where she had gone to meet her husband in January 1899. The captain married again in the next year in Cape Town. Elizabeth Hughes had been the headmistress at the boarding school in Carnarvon, now known as Caernarfon, in North Wales. She arrived in South Africa, along with the captain's daughter Kate Pritchard, on the ship *Garth Castle* for the wedding. The *North Wales Express* said the wedding had been a big celebration in October 1900: "There was bunting in the bay in honour of the event and considerable rejoicings in shipping circles, Captain Barlow-Pritchard being one of the most popular skippers in port. The happy couple, who were warmly congratulated by hosts of friends, were presented with a magnificent wedding cake, 3ft. in height, by the captain and officers of the 'Garth Castle.'"

Captain Thomas Pritchard was from a family of seafarers based in the port town of Carnarvon, as it was then called. His brother Owen captained the sailing bark *Haddon Hall* and their father had been captain of *Prince Llewelyn*. Many of their officers and crew were from the area as well, so the Welsh newspaper archives contain a wealth of information about their travels.

The following year, *Glenesslin* was blocked from leaving port in San Francisco when a union strike in the summer of 1901 kept dozens of vessels carrying grain from being loaded. On September 27, 1901, the *San Francisco Call* reported "the blockade of the grain fleet has been broken and a fleet of seven vessels will be on its way East and to Europe by Saturday morning. The British ships *Celtic Monarch* and *King Edward,* fully loaded and manned, got away yesterday, while the *Dovenby, Mooltan, Glenesslin, Foyledale* and the American ship *William F. Babcock* will sail tomorrow morning."

It was a time of change in the United States. Workers were seeking better treatment and wages throughout the country. President McKinley had just been assassinated earlier that month on September 14, and Teddy Roosevelt was the new president. President Roosevelt would soon negotiate the building of the Panama Canal. When built, the canal would bring a great change to international shipping. The amount of time it took for ships to travel between the Atlantic and Pacific Oceans would be vastly shorter once ships could cross through a narrow portion of Central America instead of going all the way around the horn of South America.

Glenesslin was involved in a friendly racing rivalry with other similar ships. The average sail time from San Francisco to the UK at that time was one hundred days. *Glenesslin* is recorded as having made the journey in seventy-four days on one occasion. The *San Francisco Call* described the current wager after the lifting of the grain blockade: "Captain Pritchard of the *Glenesslin* has wagered a new suit of clothes with Captain Newman of the *King Edward* that his ship will be home first in spite of the two days' start which the *King Edward* has. The captains of the *Dovenby*, *Mooltan*, *Glenesslin* and *Foyledale* have agreed to purchase the best pair of marine glasses in England for the captain of the winning ship." According to the book *The Last of the Windjammers*, *Glenesslin* won the race by seventeen days.

Sadly, the new wife of Captain Pritchard died while traveling with her husband too, in May 1903 according to the *North Wales Express*. "News reached Carnarvon on Friday of the death at Lourenco Marquez (*sic*), Delagoa Bay, South Africa, of Mrs. Barlow-Pritchard, wife of Captain Barlow-Pritchard, of the ship 'Glenesslin.'" The newspaper had just received a letter from her describing their arrival in the harbor and her impressions of the area, today known as Maputo, Mozambique. "A melancholy interest attaches to the following letter which we received this week: —Ship 'Glenesslin,' Lourenco Marquez (*sic*), Delagoa Bay, May 9, 1903.—Just a few words about Delagoa Bay, which, perhaps, you may be glad to receive. As this is my husband's first visit here he felt rather anxious about getting into the place." Details of her death are not clear, but Elizabeth Pritchard did go on to hint that the water was perhaps unsanitary. "At present, it being winter, the climate is not so unhealthy, but still the heat is very intense, and the summer here must be very unhealthy, owing to the present very unsatisfactory state of the sewerage."

In the early twentieth century, the age of sail was nearing its end. Historical records hint that it was becoming more difficult to keep good, qualified crews on large sailing ships.[1] Many young officers trained on sailing ships for a few years and then moved to steamships. Gerald Norman Jones joined *Glenesslin* in 1902 as an apprentice. He had become fascinated with sailing ships in the harbor as a child in Holyhead, UK, and joined the ship in Liverpool. Once his service on *Glenesslin* was up, he said, "I was now faced with the problem of putting in the remainder of my time for the second mate's certificate. I did not wish to go in a sailing ship for fear of shipping for a longer voyage than anticipated." Jones switched to steamships and later worked for White Star Line. He was scheduled on the passenger liner *Titanic*, but got transferred before that ship made her fateful, lone crossing. He rose through the ranks to become Commodore Gerald N. Jones CBE, DSO, RD, RNR.

In December 1903, Captain Pritchard was caught up in a monetary scandal that took unfair advantage of some of his sailors. When *Glenesslin* arrived in Portland, the keeper of a local boardinghouse enticed a number of sailors to abandon their ship. The captain admitted to paying the keeper $20 for each of the seven sailors who had quit the crew. The keeper was then paid $35 each for recruiting replacement sailors before *Glenesslin* left port. The practice was called crimping. Due to the wages forfeited by the sailors, and by not having to pay boarding costs for the sailors while in port, the captain saved a lot of money in the racket. Pritchard left the ship not long afterward.[2]

Glenesslin continued racing her cargo around the world. There were fewer and fewer large windjammers to compete with by that time. By 1913, Captain Owen Williams, formerly master of the British bark *Port Stanley*, was in command of *Glenesslin*. The three-masted sailing ship was twenty-eight years old.

On Wednesday, October 1, 1913, *Glenesslin* and its crew of twenty-one approached the Oregon coast for the last time. It had been a slow journey. The ship had been at sea for 125 days out of Brazil and was carrying no cargo, only an 850-ton ballast of rubble or sand. She was headed for the Columbia River to pick up a load of wheat in Portland. "We had tried to make the trip to Portland by way of the Horn," one of the sailors later reported, "but contrary winds made this impossible, so we put about and made the passage around the Cape of Good Hope." So instead of sailing around the tip of South America and up the west coast, the ship had sailed across the Atlantic, around the southern tip of Africa, and then all the way across the Indian and Pacific Oceans to reach Oregon.

The ship was moving north and east toward the mouth of the Columbia River. The crew had spotted the light of the Tillamook Rock Lighthouse, about thirteen miles north of Neahkahnie Mountain, at around 8:00 p.m. the previous night. The Tillamook Rock Lighthouse sits atop a rocky island one mile off the shore of Tillamook Head. The first-order Fresnel lens of the lighthouse could be seen at a range of twenty-one miles in good clear weather. The crew spotted the coast, which was hazy that day according to the captain, at approximately 11:00 a.m.

At about noon, the ship was twenty miles offshore and still at least thirteen miles south of Tillamook Rock Lighthouse. Captain Williams set a course for shore in fair seas and five-knot winds out of the north and then went to take a short nap. He had been up the previous two nights leading up to the day of the shipwreck and had left instructions to be called at 2:00 p.m. so he could supervise turning the ship north into the wind, away from shore. He planned to maneuver the ship slightly seaward, keeping the shore in sight before turning back east toward the Columbia River Lightship. He wanted to keep an eye on the coast, given the tendency for fog to suddenly develop at this time of year.

It is here the accounts of what happened next begin to differ. The second mate, twenty-two-year-old John Colefield, was on watch. Colefield said he notified the captain that they were getting close to the shore at 1:55 p.m. and again at 2:05, but was told to come back at 2:30 p.m. The second mate also called the first mate, L. W. Howarth, who was resting as well, several times before the first mate finally roused the captain. Captain Williams, by contrast, claimed he was not called until well after 2:00 p.m., when the first mate updated him of their position. Either way, by the time the captain made it up on deck, the ship was already in danger.

The winds were coming down from the north, which is the direction *Glenesslin* would need to turn toward the Columbia River. A ship cannot sail directly into the wind and must make a series of "tacking" or "wearing" maneuvers instead, zigzagging and looping across the wind to reach the desired position. Depending on the winds, seas, and currents, a ship could get stuck during tacking maneuvers, bow to the wind and going nowhere. This is referred to as the ship being "in irons." Wearing a ship is a much less complicated maneuver. Rather than heading directly into the wind, the ship makes a wide loop or series of loops instead, turning at first in the opposite direction from the wind.

First mate Howarth had difficulty getting the crew to work the rigging fast enough to tack the ship back out to sea. The ship was able to turn north, but it was too close to shore, and a rocky headland was sticking out from the coast in front of them. The crew also did not have enough sea room to wear around away from the wind shadow caused by the headland. *Glenesslin* was headed straight for Neahkahnie.

Neahkahnie Mountain is a basaltic headland of jagged sea cliffs reaching over 1,600 feet high. The name means "place of the supreme deity" in the native Tillamook language. The base of the mountain is surrounded by coarse sharp rocks and large round boulders. A creation story was shared in the 1930s with ethnographer Elizabeth Jacobs. Clara Pearson, a Nehalem Tillamook tribal member, said, "South Wind created the boiling breakers beneath Neahkahnie Mountain. He built a big fire, heated large round rocks, and threw them down into the water."

For anyone watching from the nearby beachside town of Manzanita that day in 1913, it must have been an incredible sight to see a huge sailing ship glide past them on a collision course with the rocks. There was nothing the bystanders could do but watch, hoping the ship might be able to turn in time to avoid the disaster that was about to unfold. *Glenesslin* was not able to get the winds it needed to steer away from the torrid breakers in time. She slammed into the rocks of Neahkahnie, gashing open her riveted iron hull. The cargo hold immediately began to take on water. For some who witnessed the disaster and its aftermath, the wreck personified the end of a romanticized age of great sailing ships.

No one was hurt during the impact and the crew was able to send a line onto the rocks, where it was secured by the owner of a local tavern in Manzanita, S. G. Reed. Reed, along with his clerk Walter Cain and two other men, Steele and McFarland, rushed to help. They made it out over the cumbersome large round boulders to reach the scene of the wreck. A team from the Tillamook Lifesaving Crew also hurried to the area by train when they heard about the wreck, but the twenty-one officers and crew had already made it to shore.

Glenesslin *on the rocks. Note the line going to shore.* **Courtesy of Columbia River Maritime Museum, Astoria**

When questioned soon after the wreck by the local press, Captain Williams would not answer how they came to be so near the rocks. When asked who was at the helm, he said it was "one of the seamen, I don't remember his name." At the inquiry ten days after the wreck, the captain laid blame on the first and second mates for the disaster. The first and second mates testified the captain had been drinking earlier that morning and implied he was still under the influence of liquor at the time of the wreck.

The Lloyd's of London insurance company surveyor based in Portland, Captain Vesey, visited the ship the day after the wreck, October 2. He determined there would be no chance to refloat her. Water was flowing freely through the hull. He recommended the ship be sold immediately.

A number of reasons were theorized as to why the large sailing ship might have run directly into the side of that mountain on a calm autumn day. We may never know the whole truth of what happened aboard *Glenesslin* leading up to the wreck on October 1, 1913. Captain Williams said there was a thick haze and heavy swells, while the weather appeared calm and clear to witnesses on shore. Regardless of the conditions, communications between the officers were clearly strained. The crew may have been less experienced than sailors of previous decades. Some witnesses on shore claimed the crew and captain were drunk. Others believed the aging ship was wrecked intentionally for the insurance money.

Steam vessels had become more economically viable for shipping companies than the aging sailing fleets. The steam engine had been in use for a long time, but it was the high-pressured triple-expansion engines, developed in the early 1880s, that took over the ocean trade and brought about the end of the age of sail. Curator Stephen Canright of the San Diego Maritime Museum succinctly describes the engine: "They used relatively high pressure steam very efficiently, cycling the steam through progressively larger diameter cylinders, at progressively lower pressures. Virtually all of the expansive potential of the steam was converted into motive force."

The large sailing cargo ships could not keep up with the faster, less weather-dependent steamships with their propeller screws and smaller crews. Many shipping companies found themselves saddled with aging sailing vessels that had not made a profit in years. In the early 1900s there was a rash of accidents believed to be insurance fraud. The well-known marine insurer, Lloyd's of London, paid the insurance claim on *Glenesslin*. The representative from Lloyd's sent to the wreck site would have been well aware of the economic circumstances and the spate of similar wrecks that pointed to fraud attempts.

Sailors often appear stumbling drunk after transitioning from living at sea for months on a moving, pitching deck back to walking on solid land. In this case, *Glenesslin* had been at sea for 125 days. Some of the local citizens claimed they smelled alcohol on the captain and many of the crew. The captain vehemently denied he was drunk and insisted he had not been drinking. However, hints persisted through the inquest that at least some of the crew had been drinking.

Glenesslin *from the bow with onlookers standing on a boulder shows the scale of the ship and the difficulty in reaching the wreck for salvage.* **Courtesy of Columbia River Maritime Museum, Astoria**

Captain Williams had an unblemished record, with more than twenty-five years at sea. He was well known in Portland and Astoria from his time as master of his previous ship, the British bark *Port Stanley*. If his officers had less experience, however, since so many officers and sailors had already transferred to the steam-powered fleets, the first and second mates of *Glenesslin* may not have been able to anticipate problems or provide the leadership needed in an intense situation. Testimony also brought to light that no changes in course were allowed without orders from the captain, who was not on deck until it was too late to save the ship.

The inquiry was gathered on October 11, where the British consul, Erskine, along with two British ship captains, Davidson and Dalton, interviewed the officers and crew of *Glenesslin*. Captain Owen Williams was charged with being "negligent in his duty" and lost his master's certificate for three months. First mate L. W. Howarth was reprimanded for not reacting quickly enough when notified of the imminent danger.

The inquiry primarily laid blame on second mate John Colefield, who was on watch leading up to the wreck, for allowing the ship to get too close to the rocks. The Chinese cook testified he tried to warn the second mate that the ship was too close to shore but was told to mind his own business. The inquiry determined the second mate should have been more insistent about getting the captain up on deck. Further, he was negligent "in not taking matters into his own hands and ordering the crew to wear ship in the critical position in which he considered the vessel to be" when his second call was not answered. Colefield lost his second mate certificate for six months.

Glenesslin was the second windjammer built in the United Kingdom to go aground near Manzanita that year. On February 13, 1913, the 283-foot *Mimi* wrecked in fog just south of Neahkahnie Mountain on nearby Nehalem Spit. She was a four-masted sailing bark built in Glasgow, originally named *Glencova*. The ship was sold to a German shipping company, where she was renamed *Mimi*. An attempt to salvage that ship in April 1913 had gone terribly wrong, resulting in at least sixteen lives lost when the ship rolled over in the surf.

View of Neahkahnie Mountain and the Glenesslin *wreck from the town of Manzanita. The flagpole in the foreground is said to be from the shipwreck* Mimi. **Courtesy of the Nehalem Valley Historical Society, Manzanita. Photographer Ward Mayer**

"Who Wants to Buy a Fairly Good Ship?" Bids were sought in the Sunday, October 5, newspapers to sell *Glenesslin* "with all tackle, apparel, furniture, and ship's stores." The advertisement claimed reports that the ship was breaking up were unfounded and that the value of the removed items and salvaged hull could fetch $10,000. The salvage rights were sold twice within a week, first for $560 and then for $100 after the original contractors saw the difficult terrain. Lew Ullfer and Henry Bell were able to reach the ship by boat. They removed sails, rigging, three lifeboats, and another small boat known as the "captain's gig." According to the local paper, two of the lifeboats were repurposed as commercial fishing boats and used in nearby Nehalem Bay.

As the winter storms began to roll in, the ship sank beneath the waves. A photograph claiming to be the last image before *Glenesslin* capsized completely and disappeared from view was dated November 15, 1913. Many of the well-known wreck photographs were signed by local businessman Ward Mayer. Mayer lived in Wheeler and was said to have owned a lumber mill in Nehalem.

A few people were able to board the once majestic ship after it wrecked, including photographer Ward Mayer, who took this image of the deck and steering gear. **Courtesy of Columbia River Maritime Museum, Astoria**

The known remains of *Glenesslin* today only consist of some rusty metal hull plating and a few objects in museums. The ship had several anchors. Two were reportedly salvaged by Bert Gresham by pulling them up the side of the mountain with an engine used for logging

Possible last image of Glenesslin *before the ship capsized.* **Courtesy of Columbia River Maritime Museum, Astoria. Photographer Ward Mayer, dated November 15, 1913**

known as a steam donkey, but their locations are unknown.³ A bell with the name *Glenesslin* went to the Tillamook Pioneer Museum, and several metal pieces ended up at the Nehalem Valley Historical Society. A scrapbook made out of sailcloth from the ship is in the archives at the Columbia River Maritime Museum.

A photo of *Glenesslin* filled an entire page of the *Sunday Oregonian* magazine section a week after the wreck. The caption reads, in part, "From the South Seas to the colder climes, from the Oriental to the European Continents, she has voyaged. . . . Hereafter she will fill the niche principally of a curiosity for beach residents and those who 'take' the trail between Nehalem and Seaside, who may stand on the top of Necarney and gaze down on the rotting decks of what had once been the home of men and bearer of goods valued at many millions."

It is dangerous to access the pieces of metal hull remnants on the rocks, so site visits are not recommended. The Maritime Archaeological Society team hiked out to the site at the lowest tide of the summer on a clear, calm day and had to navigate over and around countless large boulders. It is possible to see a couple of the larger pieces of iron by

Large pieces of riveted iron tumbled in the Neahkahnie rocks. **Courtesy of the Maritime Archaeological Society. Photographer Jennifer Kozik**

Riveted iron partially buried in rocks at the base of Neahkahnie Mountain. **Courtesy of the Maritime Archaeological Society. Photographer Harvey Schowe**

carefully looking down from the Neahkahnie viewpoint along Highway 101. As far as the rest of the ship, portions may remain underwater in the breakers near the base of Neahkahnie, or some may have floated out to settle offshore nearby, just waiting to be discovered.

Jennifer Kozik

IOWA

HURRICANE-FORCE WINDS AND TRAGEDY ON PEACOCK SPIT, 1936

Storm warnings had been posted when the freighter SS *Iowa* set out for San Francisco from Astoria late on the night of Saturday, January 11, 1936. The weather may have seemed favorable when the steamship left Astoria with her crew of thirty-four, but a high wind soon began whipping up toward hurricane-force levels at seventy-two miles per hour. The ship was spotted by lookouts at Point Adams and Cape Disappointment as she headed into the Columbia River Bar. *Iowa* never made it out. By the time the storm subsided, her masts were all that remained above water.

Earlier that day, the freighter left Weyerhaeuser pier in Longview, Washington, and headed downstream. *Iowa* stopped in Astoria to drop off river pilot Captain Stewart V. Winslow. The pilotage that day was routine for Winslow. "I have seen much worse conditions," he said. The two aft holds at the back of the ship were fully loaded with canned salmon, fruit, flour, matches, and shingles. The remaining two forward holds were empty, reserved for cargo to be picked up in California. Two million board feet of lumber were held on the main deck. When the ship left Astoria, she headed downriver toward the Pacific Ocean, bound for San Francisco. From there, *Iowa* would head for the Panama Canal and New York.

The freighter *Iowa* was captained by Portland resident Edgar L. Yates. Originally from England, Yates was an experienced master, with papers that included the Columbia River entrance. He was licensed to pilot the Columbia River Bar and had done so on numerous occasions during his service with the States Steamship Company, which owned the ship. This was his first trip as master of *Iowa*, however. Sixty-eight-year-old Yates was supported by a crew of thirty-two Americans plus one Canadian. They were diverse in background and experience, and a majority of them lived in the Pacific Northwest. They included a chief engineer; radio operator; first, second, and third assistant engineers; deck engineer; first, second, and third mates; chief and second cooks; a wiper; a steward; two mess men; a mess boy; three oilers; nine seamen; three firemen; a boatswain; and a carpenter.

Iowa was originally designed as a naval auxiliary vessel to support the First World War. Hostilities ended before construction was completed, however, so the vessel was never used to support the war effort. Instead,

Note the bygone States Steamship Company logo on the funnel of Iowa. *Swastikas were a common symbol used worldwide prior to World War II.* **Courtesy of the Columbia Pacific Heritage Museum, Ilwaco**

the ship carried cargo for several companies. Originally named SS *West Cadron*, the ship was completed in 1919 as a service freighter by the Western Pipe and Steel Company in San Francisco. She was one of eighteen standard type 1019 design steel-hulled cargo ships constructed between 1919 and 1920 for the United States Shipping Board, or USSB. All of the ships in that line started with the name *West*.

According to the *Dictionary of Nautical Acronyms*, civilian merchant vessels traditionally begin with a prefix based on their mode of propulsion. Steamships get the prefix SS, sailing vessels use SV, paddle steamers use PS, and motor vessels get MV. If *West Cadron* had been a US military ship during the war, it would have had the USS prefix, for United States ship, which denotes ownership by the United States.

A large fleet of vessels were built for the USSB to carry troops and materials during the war. After the war this fleet was surplused and repurposed. Henry Ford bought 199 of the vessels in 1925 to study how the vessel materials could be reused. Many were used for trade in peacetime with the US Merchant Marine fleet. All American-flagged commercial vessels are considered part of the merchant marine fleet,

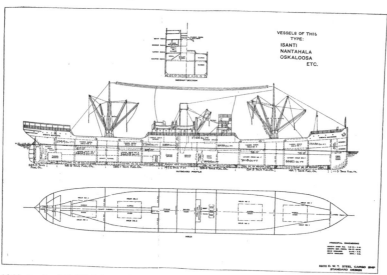

1019 standard USSB design style. **Courtesy of the United States Shipping Board, 1920**

regardless of whether the ships are civilian or federally owned. Crews and officers need papers and ratings from the US government. This is regulated through the US Coast Guard for the Department of Transportation.

Shortly after *West Cadron* was built, Congress passed the Merchant Marine Act. Section 27 of the Merchant Marine Act is better known as the Jones Act because it was introduced by Senator Wesley Jones. The Jones Act regulates shipping between American ports. Foreign vessels could still bring cargo to a single American port, but only American vessels could carry cargo or perform cabotage, coastwise trade, between multiple American ports. To qualify for trade between American ports, the vessel had to be built in America, be owned by an American or by an American company, and be crewed by American or naturalized sailors. The Jones Act protected the surplus vessels built at the end of World War I and the jobs of the mariners who served on them by guaranteeing commercial opportunities. It also kept a large fleet available to repurpose for national defense if needed. A number of sister ships of *West Cadron* went on to serve in convoy duty during World War II more than twenty years later. Some sister ships were sunk by German U-boats.

West Cadron was purchased from the USSB and put to use in trade by the Columbia Pacific Shipping Company. In 1928 the States Steamship Company acquired the company and *West Cadron* was renamed SS *Iowa*. *Iowa* continued to sail in the trans-Pacific, hauling general cargo and lumber from West Coast ports to New York and Philadelphia. The ship was 410 feet long and had a beam of 54 feet, with riveted construction and a triple-expansion reciprocating steam engine consisting of three Scotch boilers. Welded hull plate construction did not become common in American shipbuilding until World War II. The ship had two decks and a dead weight of 8,800 tons. Two heavy lift booms, one on each side of the main deck, were used for loading and unloading cargo. When in operation, the ship could operate on either coal or oil with a cruising radius of three thousand miles from its home port in San Francisco.

During the Prohibition era in 1929, when alcohol sales were against the law, five members of the crew were arrested in San Pedro,

California. They were spotted walking through the downtown streets in the early morning hours with a large suitcase, which raised the suspicions of local authorities. Police discovered the sailors had a suitcase full of whiskey purchased in Shanghai for $1.25 a quart. They planned to sell it for $20 a quart in California.

In 1936 the country was still recovering from the Great Depression, which had begun in late 1929. Crew wages on *Iowa* varied widely based on experience, responsibility, and skill set. Captain Yates earned the highest wage on board at $314.15 per month, while the lowest wage earner, mess boy Allan McCaughan from South Tacoma, made only $44.69 per month. The average monthly salary for US citizens at that time was $125.

As *Iowa* proceeded downriver toward the Pacific Ocean from Astoria just after midnight on Sunday, January 12, in 1936, on what would be her final journey, strong winds ranged from forty to over seventy miles per hour. The storm warnings had been in place for thirty-six hours. Knowing the warnings, Captain Yates made his fateful decision. He would take the ship out over the Columbia River Bar in spite of the worsening conditions.

As *Iowa* headed for the bar, the lookout at Point Adams reported seeing the ship at 12:30 a.m. The freighter entered the bar at about 1:30 a.m. As the weather kicked up into a squall, the Point Adams lookout lost sight of the vessel. Strong winds whipped rapidly, pounding the ship fiercely from the southwest. Weather conditions had deteriorated into some of the worst of the winter. *Iowa* was pushed out of the main navigational river channel northward by the wind.

On the north side of the three-mile-wide mouth of the Columbia River lies the dangerous coastal land formation known as Peacock Spit. The north breakers and shallow sands of the spit on the Washington side of the river have doomed many ships, including the USS *Peacock* in 1841 for which it was named, *Rosecrans* in 1913, *Laurel* in 1929, and *Admiral Benson* in 1930, among many others.

At 3:45 a.m. the radio operator on board *Iowa* sent out a call that the ship was in trouble near Peacock Spit. *Iowa* struck the spit and became stranded about a half mile above the north jetty and a mile and a half from shore. The force of the impact tore away the load of lumber and lifeboats from the main deck. Nino Sunseri was a meteorologist at the North Head Lighthouse weather station, just north of Cape Disappointment on the headlands at the north side of the Columbia River. He and the others at the station looked for the ship through a telescope.

The US Coast Guard cutter *Onondaga*, under the command of Captain R. Stanley Patch, headed out into the huge swells to help the ship and tried, unsuccessfully, to get close enough to shoot a rescue line.[1] The freighter was rapidly breaking up. Patch later recounted, "A few moments after we first sighted the wreck, the stash and bridge went over the side." From the lighthouse, Sunseri reported seeing two sets of flags raised by the ship shortly after daybreak, but it was too difficult to read them from his vantage point above. Charles Hubbard, assistant meteorologist at North Head, said he could see a man climbing a ladder of the ship at about the same time. Hubbard reportedly witnessed the pilothouse, funnel, and bridge getting washed away. It must have been an unreal scene to witness through a telescope.

Back on *Onondaga*, Patch said, "An hour later all that could be seen was the foremast and part of the forecastle. Three men appeared clinging to the rigging and then were seen no more." Waves pounded *Onondaga*, injuring their electrician, Stilwell, as well as damaging ventilators, stanchions, and two deck boats. The vessel had no choice but to return to port and wait for the weather to improve.

A coast guard Douglas amphibian plane from Port Angeles flew over the wreck site later that morning. They reported seeing no survivors. Cargo from the broken ship littered the water around the wreck site. Lifeboats from Point Adams and Cape Disappointment both tried to reach the damaged vessel in search of survivors, but they were unable to get within a mile of the wreck. The storm finally lessened by dusk.

Captain Lars Bjelland from the Point Adams Coast Guard Station later reported he believed the freighter struck the sand on Peacock Spit with such force that she immediately broke into two pieces. When the ship broke, the aft, or rear, section likely rolled and entered deep

Only a mast and part of the forecastle remained visible the next day. **Courtesy of the Columbia River Maritime Museum, Astoria**

water while the bow was forced northward in the sand. The ship had been damaged once before, in 1934, in a collision with the *Heiyei Maru No. 12* off Hakodate, Japan, and required major repairs. There would be no saving the ship this time.

A search team of 250 volunteers from the Civilian Conservation Corps stationed at Fort Canby combed a twenty-eight-mile stretch of shoreline from McKenzie Head at Cape Disappointment to Leadbetter Point at the northern end of Long Beach Peninsula. The Civilian Conservation Corps, or CCC, employed several million young men from around the country as part of the New Deal. The men in the CCC made $30 a month, of which they had to send home $25. CCC crews built Oregon Coastal Highway 101, set up erosion suppression around local jetties, and improved public parks all over Oregon and Washington. Crews were stationed near Fort Stevens on the Oregon side and Fort Canby on the Washington side.

In addition to the Fort Canby CCC search for the lost *Iowa* crew, a watchman hired by the owners of the States Steamship Company patrolled the shoreline from Cape Disappointment and Nahcotta daily, watching for bodies that may have washed onto the beach. Lumber and other cargo washed up on the beaches north of the mouth of the river as far as one hundred miles away from where the ship sank. Canned salmon, shingles, and flour that had spilled from the aft cargo holds as the ship broke up littered the nearby beaches.

Of the thirty-four individuals on the vessel, only ten bodies were ever found. Among the recovered remains were those of twenty-eight-year-old carpenter Marion J. Perich. He lived in Portland and was originally from Austria. His body was the first to be identified. Discharge papers from his last ship, SS *Sixola*, were still in his pocket. Forty-year-old third assistant engineer Charles Ogan from Hawaii was also found. He was a veteran of World War I, married, and had been residing in Los Angeles.[2]

The US Coast Guard's Captain Bjelland reported that two of the recovered bodies from the ship were wearing little clothing. The bodies had been thrashed by pounding waves. Bjelland believed the crew members may have been trapped in the aft section that broke off from the ship with little chance to escape.

A formal investigation was demanded after the sinking of the freighter, which took the lives of all on board. Grieving families of some of the lost crewmen joined maritime unions and the *Oregon Journal* in calling for an inquiry into whether the deceased captain had been negligent in attempting to cross the bar without a pilot. Crew members from five maritime unions were on board *Iowa* when it went down. The unions charged that profits rather than safety had guided the disastrous decision of the captain. In response to the requests, Oregon governor Charles Martin called for a thorough investigation of the sinking of *Iowa*.

What followed was an extensive twenty-eight days and thirteen nights of hearings conducted by the US Bureau of Marine Inspection and Navigation under the direction of J. B. Weaver and held in Portland, Oregon, at the US District Courthouse. Because there were no survivors to provide information, testimony included three bar pilot captains who stated that they would not have taken the ship out in such rough seas. The investigation was completed on February 6, 1936, and a report was issued. The report stated that "no evidence was found to support the claims that the *Iowa* was dangerously loaded with excessive stern drag and that the steering gear, engines, and compasses were out of order, or that the ship was underpowered."

The commissioner ruled the ship was under no obligation to bring a bar pilot on board because Captain Yates was a competent shipmaster. Ultimately, Captain Yates was blamed for the loss of the ship and the lives of the thirty-three crewmen who served under him. Despite objections filed by the Yates estate and other claimants over the findings, the captain was found to be negligent in trying to sail through the storm. District Judge James Alger Fee said the recklessness of the captain was the sole cause of the disaster.

The States Steamship Company was found to have failed to provide a Notice to Mariners advising of hazards including the loss of two buoys and the light on a third buoy. The report also noted that the ship did not have the required communication system between the bridge and engine room. Although the finding would have rendered the SS *Iowa* unseaworthy, neither the communications issue nor missing buoys had caused the sinking of the ship according to the commissioner. On March 12, the States Steamship Company filed a successful petition for exoneration and a limit of liability for the loss of life and cargo. The petition sought protection from a federal statute enacted in 1851, which limited liability to $10,624.76. The total amounted to less than $60 per ton of cargo. Seven estates of lost crew members and thirty cargo stakeholders challenged the petition, saying the amount was grossly inadequate. The thirty-seven claimants were not successful, and ultimately received either nothing or very little after expenses.

The remains of the ship completely disappeared under the waves, but they were not lost forever. Multi-beam sonar scans conducted by the US Army Corps of Engineers identified what appears to be a segment of *Iowa*. The sonar system is used to map the riverbed. It emits sound waves from beneath the hull of a vessel to produce fan-shaped coverage of the bottom. Data is collected through the measurement and recording of the time it takes for the acoustic signal to travel from the

Multi-beam view of a portion of Iowa. **Courtesy of the Army Corps of Engineers research vessel RV Elton**

transmitter to the seafloor, or an object, and back to the receiver. The Army Corps of Engineers routinely conducts multi-beam sonar in the Columbia River to make sure the navigational channel stays clear for large cargo vessels and cruise ships.

Multi-beam sonar analysis identified what appears to be near the middle of the ship. The image appears to show the area of the ship containing the three boilers and part of the two forward cargo holds, along with the engines. Other parts of the bow section of the ship may be there as well, buried in sediment and not visible in the multi-beam sonar. The identity of the submerged section of *Iowa* was confirmed by the Maritime Archaeological Society. The multi-beam image was scaled and overlaid onto a construction drawing containing the three boilers. The images line up perfectly.

The location of the aft section of the ship and its condition remains unknown. It may contain preserved cargo or even entombed remains of some of the lost crewmen depending on how deeply the section is buried in the sand. More of the ship may be nearby, buried in the sand. The known portion of *Iowa* wreckage containing the three boilers is partially buried in sediments on the seafloor of Peacock Spit in forty to

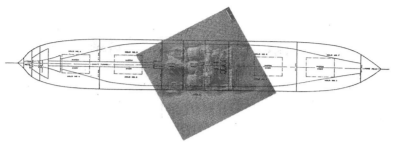

Composite of construction drawing and ortho view.

fifty feet of water. The freighter was an iron ship, which is susceptible to deterioration from physical processes such as waves, currents, and sediment abrasion as well as chemical processes.

The Columbia Pacific Heritage Museum in Ilwaco, Washington, is less than two and a half miles from the North Head Lighthouse, where weathermen watched the wreck of *Iowa* unfold. On display at the museum is a ship log from *Iowa*. Logs were like an odometer at sea. Revolutions of the spinning metal point at one end of the rope, which

Artifact from the wreckage of Iowa. **Courtesy of the Columbia Pacific Heritage Museum, Ilwaco. Photographer Jennifer Kozik**

was pulled behind the ship, translated to knots on the gauge at the other end of the rope on board.

The story of *Iowa* seems to be included in every book that touches on the history of the Columbia River Bar. In many ways *Iowa* was just an ordinary cargo vessel, one of many passing by Astoria every day. Yet it grabs the imagination. With thirty-four men lost, *Iowa* was the largest maritime disaster on the bar since forty-two people lost their lives on the sternwheeler *General Warren* in 1852. The photograph with just the mast of *Iowa* sticking above water, showing members of the coast guard in the foreground looking for survivors, is an iconic view. Even more than eighty years later, the wreck of the freighter *Iowa* remains one of the most well-known tragedies of the Columbia River Bar.

Jim Sharpe

TRINIDAD

TREACHEROUS RESCUE AND A CURIOUS WANDERING SHIPWRECK, 1937

Floating wreckage of an old ship came to rest on the beach just north of Willapa Bay in November 2016. The mysterious wooden frame was known by locals to have vanished and reappeared a number of times around Washaway Beach, Washington. First noticed in late 2009 near North Cove, the wreckage eroded out of a crumbling sandy hillside. Once free, it began to move south and rotate with the tides, its timbers entangling old fishing nets, bull kelp, and other debris in the turgid waters.

The winter storm season had already begun to settle on the coast when the Maritime Archaeological Society, in cooperation with the Westport South Beach Historical Society, set out to survey the nearly one-hundred-foot by twenty-foot wreckage at low tide before it disappeared again. In the short time before the tide rolled back in, the team ran a baseline using a tape measure along the length of the ship. They took measurements and photographs of the ship while looking for diagnostic details that might help identify the vessel. Often, there is not much else a shore-based research team can do. It is not feasible to move

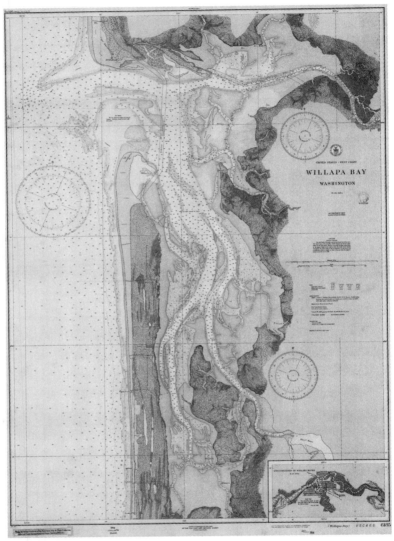

Map of Willapa Bay and Washaway Beach, historically known as Cape Shoalwater. **Courtesy of the National Oceanic and Atmospheric Administration, Historical Map & Chart Collection**

heavy, unstable wreckage to higher ground. Even if it could be secured, the wood and metal would quickly deteriorate once it began to dry.

The entrance to Willapa Bay, formerly known as Shoalwater Bay, is between Grays Harbor to the north and the mouth of the Columbia River to the south. Willapa Bay is separated from the Pacific Ocean by Long Beach Peninsula, which is a low sand spit extending twenty-eight miles north from Cape Disappointment. The northern shoulder of the entrance to the bay was historically called Cape Shoalwater. At least twenty ships are known to have wrecked near the north end of Willapa Bay, including the wooden steam lumber schooner *Trinidad* in 1937. *Trinidad* may be associated with the ghostly, roaming remains of the mysterious vessel.

The steamship *Trinidad* left Raymond, Washington, bound for San Francisco with a crew of twenty-two and a full load of lumber on Friday, May 7, 1937. Under the command of Captain Ingvald Hellesto, the ship steamed out of the Willapa River toward the Willapa Bay Bar. *Trinidad* was a 974-ton coastal lumber steamer built by Hammond Lumber Company with a Union Iron Works 600-horsepower triple-expansion engine. She was launched from the Bendixsen shipyard in Fairhaven, California, in 1917 and was soon followed by a sister ship named *Halco*. These small wooden steam schooners, ranging from ninety to just over two hundred feet in length, dominated the lumber trade along the West Coast in the late nineteenth and early twentieth centuries. *Trinidad* was approximately 210 feet long with a 42-foot-wide beam and a 14-foot hold depth. The ship had the capacity to hold 1.2 million board feet of lumber.

These maneuverable ships were built to haul lumber in and out of the less accessible ports along the West Coast. They were, however, vulnerable to the Pacific Ocean storms along the lee shore of the coast. Several hundred steam lumber schooners were built. Some ended up smashed on the beaches or rocks along the coast. Others were beaten to pieces by huge waves driven by gale-force winds as they tried to keep balanced the tons of lumber strapped to their decks. *Halco*, the sister ship of *Trinidad*, ended her career stranded on a beach outside of Grays Harbor, Washington, in 1925 and was sold for salvage.

The entrance channel was in the northern part of Willapa Bay. The beaches there are infamously known for having the fastest-eroding coastline on the West Coast, losing a hundred feet of shoreline or more in some spots each year. By 1937, the Willapa Bay Lighthouse, which had guided ships since 1858, was precariously close to the edge of a crumbling cliff. The nearby Willapa Bay Coast Guard Station was located just inside Cape Shoalwater on North Cove. Both of these landmarks are gone today, along with other parts of the town, eroded into the sea. The shallow Willapa Bay Bar is now only crossed by locals with detailed knowledge of the channel.

On that day in 1937, a storm was picking up. It turned into a gale as evening approached. *Trinidad* struggled to cross the Willapa Bay Bar for over two hours in the huge seas and gale-force winds. The seams of the ship began to open. The crew worked the pumps, trying to stay ahead of the sea pouring into the ship. Captain Hellesto could no longer keep the ship on course in the channel. *Trinidad* struck the sands of Cape Shoalwater between Buoys 6 and 7. The captain of the wooden steam schooner immediately ordered the engines reversed in an attempt to back off the sands. The next huge wave slammed the *Trinidad* down on the sand so hard that the engine parted from its mounts, breaking the steam piping in the process.

Trinidad was stranded about a mile west of Willapa Bay Lighthouse, dead in the water with no power. Each successive wave smashed against the steamship, pressing her farther onto the sand. *Trinidad* was not equipped with a radio to call for help. At 8:15 p.m., Captain Hellesto launched flares to signal distress. Red trails of light briefly lit up the night sky, one after the other. The sight was eerie for crew member George Millen. He said, "It was raining to beat hell, and it kind of gave you the creeps to see those flares go arching up into nothing and then leave the night blacker than ever."

The ship was beginning to show signs of breaking up. Lashings for the lumber snapped, and cargo began rolling off the ship. Second mate

Warner Kraft attempted to launch a small boat and lead the evacuation, but the relentless swells smashed the craft against the hull of the ship. "We got one boat over the side," Millen recalled, "but it no more than touched the water when it went to pieces like a matchbox." Kraft was washed overboard, and the crew never saw him alive again. The captain and the rest of the crew took shelter in the wheelhouse. There was nothing they could do but hope someone had seen their flares.

The Willapa Bay Coast Guard Station watchtower did see the red streaks of the distress flares. Unfortunately, their rescue ship, a motor lifeboat, was already at sea on another emergency call from a fishing vessel. Willapa Bay called north for help from the Grays Harbor station in Westport.

Fourteen miles to the north, at the Westport Coast Guard Station, the USCG crews had been performing routine maintenance tasks and conducting practice drills. Boatswain's mate Hilman John Persson, the head of the station, was a thirty-year veteran of the lifesaving service and coast guard. He noted the winds had turned from a light breeze into heavy gusts. When the call came in about a ship in need of help, he quickly gathered a crew to take their motor lifeboat south to Willapa Bay. Accompanying boatswain Persson were motor mechanics Roy Anderson and Jesse Mathews as well as surfmen Roy Woods and Daniel Hamalainen. For Hamalainen, this would be his first rescue mission.

Boatswain's mate is a rating, or job title, in the US Coast Guard and Navy. A boatswain (pronounced "bosun") is an expert in rigging, deck equipment, and small boat operations. On a sailing ship, a boatswain would start out learning to maintain and operate the deck equipment, rigging, and anchors. On a steamship, a boatswain would operate and maintain the decks, funnels, and other equipment not covered by the engineers. As a boatswain's mate gains experience and rank, he or she would become a noncommissioned officer in charge of these duties.

It is not uncommon in the coast guard for chief petty officer boatswain's mates to be in command of small units. A noncommissioned officer who holds a command is referred to as the officer in charge. Persson was promoted from chief petty officer to warrant officer in

1930, making him the commanding officer of the station. He would be referred to as "Captain," as that is an honorific title for the commander of a station regardless of rank.

It took the five men in the thirty-six-foot Grays Harbor motor lifeboat, *MLB 3829*, an hour and a half to cross the bar at Grays Harbor and turn south into the gale for the fourteen-mile trip down the coast in the dark. In addition to the sixty-mile-per-hour winds and relentless swells, they had to contend with a strong northward current. Persson instructed the four other members of the crew to watch for signals coming from either the stranded ship or the Willapa Bay motor lifeboat. He climbed into the small forward cabin to monitor the radio. Before leaving the station at Westport, Persson had left instructions for the station to call them every fifteen minutes with updates on the weather and the stranded vessel.

MLB 3829 was a Type TR rescue craft built in 1932. These thirty-six-foot motor lifeboats were a mainstay of the coast guard lifesaving service for over fifty years, from 1929 until they were taken out of service in 1987. They were built of cypress or Port Orford cedar planking over oak frames and powered by a single gas or diesel engine driving a single propeller. The boats were self-righting and self-bailing, with five watertight compartments. They had a top speed of over eight knots and a range of 280 nautical miles. It is difficult to imagine what it would be like to roll over in such a vessel, which sometimes happens in heavy surf. In a personal communication with a modern coast guardsman who crews a self-righting motor lifeboat, he said, "When she rolls over we hold on, hold our breath, and pray."

It was a long night for the imperiled crew on *Trinidad*. The captain opened the medicine chest and brought out a bottle of whiskey. They tried to keep their spirits up, joking around while sharing the whiskey, along with bread and bologna. This would be the last in a long run of bad luck for *Trinidad*. The ship had already been involved in several collisions over the years and once had to be towed by the coast guard after the loss of a propeller.

Nearly seven hours had passed since *Trinidad* had launched her distress flares. It was 3:00 a.m. on Saturday, May 8, when the crew of *MLB 3829* spotted the stricken vessel. The steamship crew, still huddled in the wheelhouse, could see the lights of their rescuers approaching. The motor lifeboat would appear and then drop out of sight in the big waves. One *Trinidad* crew member said, "The sea was the worst I've ever seen."

Now, more lives were at stake. The storm had already destroyed one small boat when it smashed against the hull of the ship and took the life of their second mate. There was also loose lumber, rigging, and other debris in the water. It would be dangerous for rescuers in the small coast guard vessel to pull up alongside *Trinidad*, stuck in the sand with her masts swaying and high waves breaking over her side.

As the MLB got closer, Persson studied the surf and breaking waves to figure out how best to approach *Trinidad*. Just before dawn, at 5:00 a.m., the coast guard crew made their first approach attempt. A

Photo of Trinidad *from the coast guard rescue ship in stormy seas.* **Courtesy of the Westport South Beach Historical Society**

breaking wave completely submerged the motor lifeboat for a moment. With dawn, and more light, Persson noticed an oil slick from *Trinidad*'s ruptured fuel tanks partially calming the breaking waves near the ship. It could be just enough for the motor lifeboat to finally get close enough to begin taking the crew off the ship. The MLB had to maneuver itself alongside the ship again and again, rescuing a few men at a time before getting pushed away by the wind and waves.

All twenty-one remaining crew members were safely loaded onto *MLB 3829*, despite the conditions.[1] There were now twenty-six men on the thirty-six-foot vessel. Captain Persson said, "I could feel we had a heavy load, and several times had to warn the men to keep down as low as possible to the deck." They left the crumbling ship behind and headed for the channel. Captain Hellesto and the other crew members, including first mate Oscar Larsen, third mate Tom Delehanty, chief engineer J. Edblad, first assistant engineer S. Silbersky, second assistant engineer A. Nielsen, and Steward C. Rickstad, were transferred to a

Coast guard crew after the twelve-and-a-half-hour Trinidad *rescue.* **Courtesy of the Westport South Beach Historical Society**

nearby ship. *Ruth E.* took the survivors back to Raymond, Washington, where *Trinidad* had left the day before.

The exhausted crew of *MLB 3829* headed for Willapa Bay after the crew of the wooden steam schooner was safely aboard *Ruth E.* Once they made it safely back into the bay, a truck from the Westport station picked them up. Nearly thirteen hours had passed since distress flares were launched on *Trinidad* the previous evening. Captain Persson and his lifesaving crew received a lot of press and were awarded medals for their bravery in the rescue. Several newspapers around the country picked up the story of the stormy shipwreck despite the other big news that week. On the East Coast, the *Hindenburg* had crashed in New Jersey just one day earlier, on May 6, 1937.

A few hours after the crew was rescued, *Trinidad* broke up. Lumber and wreckage of the wooden ship were scattered on Willapa Beach. The body of second mate Warner Kraft was found near Grays Harbor. An inquest was set up to look into his death, calling Captain Hellesto and

Coast guard crew with Gold Lifesaving Medals. **Courtesy of the Westport South Beach Historical Society**

Wreckage of Trinidad. *Courtesy of the Westport South Beach Historical Society*

Captain Persson as witnesses. Persson and his crew were awarded Gold Lifesaving Medals on board the coast guard cutter *Onondaga*.[2] He also accepted the American Legion Medal of Valor in Washington, DC, on behalf of the MLB crew for the most outstanding act of heroism in the United States that year.

The wreckage found in 2009, which may be associated with *Trinidad,* has had quite the adventure. After eroding from the hillside, the wreckage worked its way south along Washaway Beach. Sometimes it was seemingly firmly lodged and reburied, but then the ever-shifting sands would be scraped away again, freeing the wreckage to continue its journey.

The materials and methods used in ship construction can help identify where and when a ship was built. In the case of the wandering shipwreck, it is the construction techniques and fasteners that can offer clues. The wreckage on the beach consists of wooden frames with interior ceiling planks and exterior hull planks. This construction technique is commonly known as composite or paired framed hull construction, with floor planks and ceiling planks. The wreckage has big metal bolts going all the way through the planks. The heads of the bolts were clinched, or peened, over a metal ring that looks like a modern flat washer, meaning they had been manually flattened on the top to hold the planks to the frames. Construction with threaded screws became more common starting in the 1920s, indicating this ship was more likely to have been built before that time. The keel was observed to be nineteen inches square.

Many local residents around North Cove, Washington, believed the wreckage was associated with the four-hundred-foot-long British coal-burning steamship *Canadian Exporter*, which grounded and broke up near the Willapa Bay entrance on August 1, 1921. Timbers associated with the cargo of *Canadian Exporter* began washing up with the tides in 1999. Many of the two-by-two-foot fir timbers, marked with *HRM* for the H. R. McMillan timber company, were hauled ashore and sold to reclamation and salvage companies. *Canadian Exporter* had a steel hull, however, which is inconsistent with the wreckage that washed out of the hillside.

The wandering wreckage was completely encased in sand for many years, so some steel hull should have been preserved if it was *Canadian Exporter*. There is no known record of the hull plating being salvaged. Additionally, locals also reported sometimes seeing wooden shiplap siding on the lower portions of the wandering wreckage. The lumber and wreckage may be completely unrelated. *Canadian Exporter* likely still lies offshore.

Ongoing research continues to eliminate other possible candidates for the wreckage. *Avalon* was another steam lumber schooner that partially burned at the entrance to Willapa Harbor in 1927. Research indicates *Avalon* was later refloated and scrapped. Some have even speculated the wreck could be a rum-runner barge, smuggling alcohol in from Canada during Prohibition in the 1920s. However, *Trinidad* remains the best candidate for the Washaway Beach remains. The wooden steamship was stranded the closest to where the wreck eroded out of the hillside. The Westport South Beach Historical Society, where a life ring from *Trinidad* and the Hilman John Persson collection are preserved at the Westport Maritime Museum, has been assisting the Maritime Archaeological Society with the research.

The wandering wreck of Washaway Beach, November 2016. **Courtesy of the Maritime Archaeological Society**

Side profile of the wandering wreck, November 2016. **Courtesy of the Maritime Archaeological Society**

Since the team documented the wreckage in late 2016, Westport South Beach Historical Society executive director John Shaw has been faithfully tracking the continuing story of the wreckage. It moved eight hundred yards overnight during the king tides in early 2017. In early 2018 it broke in two. The fore section moved onto the rocks along the edge of Highway 105 for a while and then settled on a nearby point; the aft section ran into an old culvert and began to break up. Shaw has carefully tracked the progress of the ever-shrinking shipwreck, noting the various frames, planks, and beams as they move down toward the Shoalwater Bay Reservation.

Without finding more of the shipwreck, it may not be possible for maritime archaeologists to ever positively identify the wandering wreckage as the remains of *Trinidad*. Soon nothing may be left of the wreckage that does exist, limiting its potential to yield more information about the past. The winter storms, high tides, and eroding coastline around Washaway Beach are a fascinating study on the impact of the forces related to shipwreck preservation. The wreckage remains a curiosity, along with the captivating story of its journey.

Jeff Groth

MAUNA ALA

THE YULE SHIP: CHRISTMAS TREES FOR HAWAII ON THE EVE OF WAR, 1941

Hawaii was a bustling place prior to American involvement in World War II. The US territory in the Pacific had witnessed a steady buildup of military resources and personnel on the island of Oahu, near Honolulu, where the Pacific fleet was based at Pearl Harbor. The sailors, soldiers, military families, and the diverse local population were well aware of the growing shadow of war. At the same time, Oahu was also an idyllic tropical island with a vibrant local culture and beautiful sandy beaches. It was early December 1941, and the holidays were approaching.

On Wednesday, December 3, the commercial Matson Line steamship SS *Mauna Ala* finished loading cargo in Seattle, Washington. The freighter headed out, steaming up through the Puget Sound and out into the Strait of Juan de Fuca. There, she slowed in Port Angeles to drop off the pilot who had navigated the ship out of the Puget Sound. *Mauna Ala* and her crew of thirty-eight then set out for the open Pacific Ocean on what would have normally been a routine ten-day voyage to Honolulu, just as the ship had done many times over the years.

YULE SHIP SAILS FOR HAWAIIAN ISLANDS

60,000 TREES TO CHEER ISLANDERS

Sixty thousand Christmas trees from the evergreen forests of Washington yesterday were on their way to Hawaii, where they will be the center of attraction at Yule festivities in many homes.

The trees are being carried as part of the deckload of the Matson Navigation Company's Christmas ship Mauna Ala, which is bound for Honolulu, Kahului and Hilo, and mark the largest shipment of its kind ever sent from the Northwest to the mid-Pacific islands.

Also aboard the Matson ship are 1,500 tons of other Christmas freight for Hawaii's holiday market, including chickens, turkeys, fruits, candies, meats and vegetables. The Mauna Ala sailed from the Union Pacific Dock early Thursday, riding deep in the water under the weight of 10,000 tons of freight. She is due in Honolulu December 14 in plenty of time for Christmas.

The Matson Navigation Company's Seattle-Hawaii Christmas ship, the Mauna Ala, yesterday was on her way to the mid-Pacific islands laden with a big cargo of holiday freight, including 60,000 Christmas trees carried on deck. The trees were cut in the evergreen forests of Washington and will be discharged in Honolulu, Kahului and Hilo. Upper: Sling loads of bundles of the trees going aboard the Mauna Ala at the Union Pacific Dock, and Capt. C. W. Saunders, master of the vessel, who will be Santa Claus to thousands of residents of Hawaii. Lower: The Mauna Ala, one of the Matson Line's general cargo carriers operating between the Pacific Northwest and Hawaii.

News clipping shows bundled trees waiting to be loaded on Mauna Ala. *Courtesy of the* Seattle Times, *1941*

Mauna Ala was dubbed the Christmas Ship, or Yule Ship, because she would be one of the last ships to arrive in Hawaii from the Pacific Northwest before the holidays. The cargo included festive staples such as turkey, ham, barrels of butter, and tins of Almond Roca. On the deck of the freighter, in front of the wheelhouse, the ship stowed some sixty thousand Christmas trees harvested from the forests surrounding Puget Sound.

The freighter was ideal for the Hawaiian Islands and American West Coast trade. *Mauna Ala* had 9,947 tons of deadweight capacity and measured 435 feet long by 54 feet wide. With three oil-burning Scotch boilers driving a three-thousand-horsepower steam engine, she could make a speed of ten knots. Originally named USS *Cannibas*, the ship was built for military auxiliary support in 1918, at the end of World War I, by the Texas Shipbuilding Company in Bath, Maine. The Matson shipping company purchased the ship in 1924 and renamed her *Mauna Ala*, which translates as "fragrant mountain" in native Hawaiian. Mauna 'Ala is the name of the Royal Mausoleum of Hawaii, the sacred burial ground of two major Hawaiian royal families, the Kalakaua and Kamehameha dynasties. The ship was US owned, so it remained part of the merchant marine fleet.

The excitement of the previous year's Christmas ship was covered in the December 12, 1940, *Honolulu Star-Bulletin*, with a photo featuring a young woman posing happily with two of the first Douglas fir Christmas trees to reach Honolulu. *Life* magazine also profiled the Pacific Fleet in Hawaii that same year, saying, "The soldiers and sailors stationed in Hawaii had a plum assignment, and the nation saw the harbor as proof of American naval power." People relaxed and swam on Waikiki Beach, and sailors in dress white uniforms posed for photographs with the locals, a mix of tourism and military presence.

December holiday preparations in 1941 were not destined to be a repeat of the previous year, however. Peace on the idyllic tropical island was soon shattered, and *Mauna Ala* would never reach her destination. The Japanese military attacked Pearl Harbor on the morning of Sunday, December 7. The next day, on Monday, December 8, President Franklin D. Roosevelt gave his now-famous speech about the bombings, declaring "a date which will live in infamy." Congress officially declared war on Japan the same day. An intense fear of an imminent invasion by Japanese forces began to spread in Hawaii and along the West Coast of the United States. America was now at war, and its pristine beaches would soon be covered with barbed wire.

Mauna Ala had been at sea for four days on the seventh of December and was some nine hundred miles past the departure point from the Strait of Juan de Fuca, Tatoosh Island. The ship was still over two thousand nautical miles from Hawaii.

The radio room on the ship was a hot and noisy place. "Sparky," as the radio operator was commonly known on ships, sat at his console listening closely for communications through his headphones. A Morse code key was kept close at hand. He could hear an ever-present, fairly loud background hum as well as incessant dits and daws of messages being passed back and forth over the radio waves.

At some point, a cable came in from Matson Navigation Company to relay official word of the attack. The radio operator most likely copied the transmission down on paper as it came in and then typed it up on a cable form. The message was then hand-delivered to the captain.

The master of *Mauna Ala* was Captain Charles Wells Saunders Jr. Captain Saunders likely read this particular message carefully to grasp the enormity of what happened and what it meant. Hawaii had been attacked by the Japanese. The captain was instructed to not continue on to Honolulu, but to turn the ship around and head for the Columbia River. He would have gone to the bridge, asking the mate to pull the appropriate chart and use it to lay out a new course. The new course was then passed to the helmsman and the ship turned around, heading back to the West Coast.

The vessel set on a course to the Columbia River Lightship. The lightship was stationed just off the coast at the mouth of the river that forms the border between Oregon and Washington. According to *The Official Chronology of the U.S. Navy in World War II* by Robert J. Cressman of the Naval Historical Center, the ship was told to head to Portland, Oregon, because of concerns about Japanese submarines lying in wait off the coast. The Columbia River was the closest mainland port to get the ship out of the open ocean as quickly as possible. Eastward bound, *Mauna Ala* set an estimated time of arrival at the Oregon coast for the evening of Wednesday, December 10.

The US military and the residents of the Oregon coast had quickly begun defensive preparations in case the Japanese were planning to attack the continental United States. Many military exercises took place around Astoria. Locals on the coast formed beach patrols, carrying shotguns and small-caliber rifles. US Coast Guard, National Guard, civilian airplanes, and airships patrolled the shore. Blackouts went into effect all along the West Coast during the war. Car and truck headlights were dimmed, and windows were covered at night. According to the *Daily Astorian* newspaper, the blackouts started on Monday, December 8, when "the lower Columbia was ordered dark at 6 pm, making this community the first blacked out on the Pacific coast and probably the first in the nation." Air raid observers were posted and communications centers were staffed twenty-four hours a day.

Approaching the coast was dangerous in the best of times, even without the dark veil of blacked-out coastline. Use of radar, GPS, and long-range navigation would not be used by merchant ships for decades. Celestial navigation was still the primary method used to determine position at sea, and weather conditions near the Oregon coast during the rainy season in December seldom provide ideal circumstances for obtaining a fix from the sun or stars. The *Mauna Ala* deck officers reportedly were able to take a good position reading at noon on December 10, and they had spotted land before sunset.

A line calculated from their noon position, or dead reckoning, would have set the ship near the Columbia River entrance, where a bar pilot from Astoria waited for them on board the pilot schooner *Columbia*. It was a misty evening and visibility was down to about one mile. Captain Saunders would have been on the bridge of *Mauna Ala* with lookouts posted, all eyes straining to see the characteristic white-over-red lights of the pilot schooner emerging from the mist.

The dead reckoning based on the sun line had given the navigator a path, but not the exact position along that course. An educated guess was made as to speed, but this too was subject to error. It was difficult to know how much a ship might be affected by wind or by the direction and strength of the moving current, which often changes near shore.

In mid-ocean, dead reckoning was sufficient, but near land, the good judgment of an experienced seaman was needed to verify their location.

The forty-one-year-old captain was just such an experienced seaman. He had worked for the shipping company since 1920, where he started as a quartermaster on ships traveling mostly between the West Coast and Hawaii. His seafaring career started at age five when he, along with his mother and two sisters, went to sea on the square-rigged sailing ship *St. Catherine*, where his father was master. His father, C. W. Saunders Sr., also worked for Matson. They worked the Philadelphia to Hawaii trade, traveling down around Cape Horn at the tip of South America. It was a particularly treacherous route, known for ferocious headwinds, blistering cold, and mountainous seas. At age ten, the junior Saunders was signed on the sailing ship *Moshulu* as a cabin boy and started earning a wage. He worked up through the officer ranks, obtaining his master's license at age twenty-six.

Mauna Ala approached the Oregon coast, searching for the lightship or the pilot schooner. In later testimony before the US Steamboat Inspection Service, Captain Saunders stated that a flashing signal light was observed by chief mate Anderson from an unidentified vessel at 6:32 p.m. with about one-mile visibility. He was not totally clear on the signal but could read "H A _ T" and concluded the signal was instructing the ship to halt. Captain Saunders reduced speed to dead slow. There was no further communication, however, so he returned to full ahead. All eyes strained to see the lights of the pilot boat, which should have emerged in the mist at any time.

The mouth of the Columbia River is three miles wide. It is bounded by the rocky basalt headlands of Cape Disappointment to the north in Washington State and by a low sandy area on the Oregon side to the south called Clatsop Spit. Captain Saunders would normally have had the advantage of the Cape Disappointment Lighthouse at the entrance to the river as well as the North Head Light up the coast and the Tillamook Light to the south. In good visibility, these would have given a good spread of aids to navigation and positions on approach. Additionally, the Columbia River Lightship normally broadcasted a radio direction finding (RDF) signal that allowed ships to set a course for the signal, taking them directly to the river entrance. On the evening of December 10, however, all of these aids were turned off.

The pilot boat *Columbia* sent out to meet the steamer would never see *Mauna Ala*. The pilot boat stayed on station, waiting. Having not seen the ship, the pilot boat eventually returned to Astoria. The Columbia River Bar pilots would have known the estimated time of arrival, either directly via a cable from the ship or from word passed on by the agent of the ship in Portland. Managing the logistics of pilots is complex and ever-changing, so the pilot boat could have returned to port for a number of reasons. It may have needed to return pilots or pick up other pilots for ships scheduled to arrive later that evening. Very little communication was available between the boat and office, so when *Columbia* went out to sea, she was likely scheduled to return at a given time regardless of whether the pilot boat had met up with its intended ship.

At 7:03 p.m. the lookout on the freighter reported "breakers dead ahead." *Mauna Ala* had missed both the blacked-out lightship and the mouth of the Columbia River on her approach. The ship was too far south. Officers from the ship later testified they had still expected the lightship to be operating normally, even with a blackout.[1]

As soon as breakers were sighted, the engine was put on emergency full astern, but the ship was too close to stop and reverse course. *Mauna Ala* plowed into the breakers and lodged in the sand. Christmas trees strapped on the deck at the front of the ship spilled into the water. The sandy shoal projecting off the headlands at the south side of the Columbia River, known as the Clatsop Spit, had seen many shipwrecks and had taken many lives.

Mauna Ala grounded about four miles south of the Columbia River entrance, and just one mile south of the remains of the 1906 wreck, *Peter Iredale*. Thirty-five years earlier, the captain of that steel and iron, four-masted British bark had run into the breakers too. *Peter Iredale* remained on the beach, much of her metal hull salvaged for the World War I effort.

On shore, the first reaction that Wednesday night in 1941 was described by local resident Margaret Gammon of Seaside as "paranoia and hysteria." The ship appeared to confirm their worst fears. "The Japanese are landing!" News quickly reached Camp Clatsop, today known as Camp Rilea, where military personnel turned on beach lights to catch sight of the invading forces. Colonel Clifton Irwin, commander of the coastal defense forces, gave orders to fire on the "enemy ship." After an initial panicked reaction that sent armed men to the beach, people realized it was a shipping accident and not an invasion by Japanese forces. Carl Kostol of the 41st Infantry Division was sent to defend the beach that night. In an oral history, located in the library collections at the Oregon Military Museum, Kostol recalled how they found out the invaders were really just Christmas trees. "Trees started rolling in and some got shot at," he said.[2]

The ship grounded a little after high tide at a tidal height of just over six feet. The crew made unsuccessful attempts to back off the sand of Clatsop Spit. Everyone waited on board, safe for the moment, hoping for help from a tug out of Astoria. All night the ship lay grounded, facing east toward land. The falling tide only ground the ship harder into the sand.

By dawn on Thursday, December 11, it was clear that this was an American merchant ship on the beach and assistance was required. The Point Adams Coast Guard Station crew went out to assist the crew off the freighter. They were able to get to the lee side of the ship in the shallow breakers, and every member of the crew was successfully rescued. The US Navy reportedly tried to suppress news about the wreck until Thursday afternoon.

As has been so often the case with Oregon weather, the ship grounded in fairly calm conditions, but as the day wore on, the winter weather worsened. Soon the ship was being pummeled by heavy seas and was doomed. The waves turned the ship sideways until she was broadside to the oncoming surf. Getting pounded by breakers, the bulkheads of the freighter began to give way. The cargo holds burst open, spilling Yuletide merchandise everywhere. The news spread quickly.

By Friday, December 12, the beach was packed with cars and people wanting to see the wreck and collect some of the expelled contents for themselves.

Mauna Ala had five cargo holds with 452,152 cubic feet of cargo space, including 5,820 cubic feet of refrigerated space. The ship had been built with a three-island design, meaning there were three areas raised higher than the main deck. At the front of the ship was the forecastle. The engine, with a large funnel for the boiler room, as well as the bridge with the wheelhouse, were in the center. The rear, or aft, section of the ship had a raised stern known as the poop deck. Hatches for the bursting cargo holds were located between the raised decks.

Locals remembered the beach strewn for ten miles with Christmas trees, fuel oil, and other items from the holiday cargo including oranges, apples, grapefruit, candy tins, tons of butter packed in wooden barrels, and silverware. The ship also carried everyday items such as flour and cross arms for telephone poles, which washed up onto shore. Everyone was allowed to openly salvage whatever they could take. James Scarborough of Gearhart and Gordon Perrigo of Seaside brought a dump truck onto the beach, retrieving a large haul of cargo to sell on the wartime-rationed market. They acquired barrels of butter, tins of Almond Roca, and some of what was said to be ten thousand turkeys and three thousand chickens, as well as crates of steak and ham. The pair sold the butter as far away as Forest Grove, Oregon, approximately seventy miles inland.

Many items from the wreckage were considered usable after they were thoroughly washed to remove the fuel oil that coated everything. The public was warned that caustic soda and arsenic in the cargo may have contaminated any foodstuffs found on the beach. Wayne Hess remembered his mother refused to cook the turkeys, so they built a huge bonfire of Christmas trees to dispose of them. Wayne Mitt, also a child at the time, remembered collecting rolls of wax paper, which his family used for a long time afterward. He also collected Eagle brand flour in paper bags. It was reported that some of the turkeys were so large that they would not fit in an oven without being cut in half.

Debris from the wreck washed up on Clatsop Spit and Sunset Beach. **Courtesy of Oregon Historical Society, Oregonian/Barcroft Media**

Christmas trees ended up being in short supply in Hawaii for the holidays in 1941. About 1,800 trees were known to have eventually made their way to Honolulu. The *Honolulu Advertiser* described the holiday as a solemn one in Hawaii after the bombings at Pearl Harbor. For people who did try to mark the occasion, Christmas lights were in violation of the blackouts and there was a ban on the sale of alcohol under the newly imposed martial law. The cargo of *Mauna Ala* had also carried newsprint for the *Honolulu Star-Bulletin*. The paper reported on December 12, 1941, that it would be necessary to reduce the size of their publication.

Grounded ships were always in danger of breaking up during Oregon coastal storms. There was an attempt by tugs to pull the freighter free, but the ship was already starting to break apart in the swells. In the days following the wreck, the ship slipped deeper into the sand while remnants of the cargo and a coating of fuel oil continued to wash up along the beach. By Sunday morning, the ship had broken in two, like a jackknifed truck, with the bow again pointing toward shore and the back half of the ship still sideways to the pummeling breakers. Five days after grounding, it was said that the ship had sunk twelve feet into the sand. At high tide, only parts of the superstructure remained above water.

Sometimes sandbars form around wrecked ships, building up sand until the ship is left high and dry at high tide. Such was the case with the nearby wreck of *Peter Iredale*. Some hoped another sandbar might develop from the beach to the newest shipwreck on Clatsop Spit, and began making plans for future salvage attempts. If the wreckage was accessible, *Mauna Ala* might be stripped for the war effort much like *Peter Iredale* during the First World War. A contract was awarded to the Columbia Salvage Company of Portland and Astoria.

The rusted remaining ribs of *Peter Iredale* are still a tourist attraction at Fort Stevens State Park on Clatsop Spit. The area made history during World War II as the only military installation in the continental United States fired upon since the War of 1812. It was shelled for sixteen minutes by a Japanese submarine known as I-25, which surfaced just south of the Columbia River entrance. The five-and-a-half-inch shells created craters as large as five feet wide but caused very little damage. The Fort Stevens commander gave orders not to fire back. The submarine eventually submerged and continued on its way. It is not known publicly whether Fort Stevens did not fire back because the sub was too far out for their guns to reach or because they did not want to give away their position. Barbed wire was placed on the beach. It looped through the remains of *Peter Iredale,* and beach access was blocked off to the public.

Local resident Wayne Hess remembered going to see the craters as a six-year-old child with his father after the shelling. He was awed by the sight and spent many nights sitting outside on the sand dunes with his brother and a high-powered telescope, waiting and watching for more flashes of light from incoming shells. Another local resident, also a child at the time, recalled being undeterred by the fact that beaches along the north Oregon coast were closed to civilians. He wrote, "My brother and I assumed the grownups were the only ones

Mauna Ala *sinking off Clatsop Spit.* **Courtesy of the Columbia River Maritime Museum,** *Astoria*

included in this edict and spent many afternoons exploring the gun placements."

A sandbar did not form around *Mauna Ala* during that December of 1941. The broken pieces of the wreck sank beneath the breakers. The ship would soon disappear completely, making salvage impossible. Most of the cargo and mementos were collected off the beach, not from the ship itself. The hazardous position prevented many scavengers from exploring the wreck before she was taken by the sea.

An official inquiry into the wreck was held in Portland by William A. Dugan and C. E. Gilman. They concluded the ship was lost due to the "unusual navigational situation brought about by the blackout." The maritime industry was already entering into a war footing, and the loss of merchant ships was considered an inevitable consequence in times of conflict. *Mauna Ala* was said to be one of the first US merchant ships lost after the United States officially entered the war. During World War II, a total of 733 merchant ships were eventually lost, taking many lives along with them. The crewmen of *Mauna Ala* were lucky to have all survived.

The American shipping company Matson received an insurance payment of $350,000 for the loss of the ship and cargo. At twenty-three years old, *Mauna Ala* was old for a merchant ship, although she would have been put to good use in the upcoming war. Matson had been in the Pacific trade since 1882 and owned thirty-nine vessels at the onset of World War II. The entire fleet of passenger liners and freighters was commandeered by the government during the war and painted gray. Matson continued to operate these ships and more during the war. At the height of the war, Matson's fleet of vessels, mostly government owned, grew to 172.

Captain Saunders returned home to his wife, Helene. He was later employed as a night mate, a shore-side person who relieves the officers on a ship to give them a break while in port. The wreck added a permanent blight to his record of a long career at sea. An internal report prepared by Captain A. G. Townsend, the marine operations manager for Matson Navigation Company, was critical of his actions leading up to the wreck.

> Although ordered under war conditions to proceed to the
> Columbia River and having had a good position at noon with
> an exact number of miles to the Columbia River Lightship,
> seeing land before dark, being stopped by a Government vessel
> by blinker to identify his ship, and having heard on the radio
> in the morning of blackouts on the Coast, Captain Saunders
> did nothing when the mileage was run or after being stopped
> for identification except to put engines full ahead until running
> on the beach, and we can only state that it surely is a case of
> poor judgment, poor navigation, and not taking even the most
> primary precautions that we have all been taught.

Several items from the ship made their way to the artifact collections of the Columbia River Maritime Museum in Astoria, Oregon. They include a Christmas candle, an Almond Roca candy tin, a wine bottle, three engine room logbooks, and a doorknob with a lock. Private First Class Douglas Gordenier, donor of the candle and tin, watched the wreck unfold from his station with binoculars. "On December 10, 1941, we had a searchlight just above the beach south of Fort Stevens. I witnessed the Mona Ala [*sic*] as it ran into the beach," he recalled.

One other item in the museum collection is a ten-foot by thirteen-inch name board spelling out "Mauna Ala." The sign was donated in 2004 after it was purchased at an auction. The donor claimed the board was displayed for many years at a bar in Seaside, Oregon, called Captain Morgans Restaurant. There was no information regarding how the artifact made it to the restaurant, whether it had been ripped from the wreckage or was found washed up on the beach. Before the wreck, the name board had been affixed on the top of the wheelhouse. One edge of the board was damaged and showed evidence of a repair, indicating that it may have torn from the wreckage and drifted ashore.

Almond Roca candy tin found on the beach. **Courtesy of the Columbia River Maritime Museum, Astoria. Photographer Matthew R. Palmgren**

Name board from the wheelhouse. **Courtesy of the Columbia River Maritime Museum, Astoria. Photographer Matthew R. Palmgren**

From an archaeological perspective, any remaining wreckage is likely still about four miles south of the Columbia River entrance, or one mile south of *Peter Iredale*. The largest pieces of the ship are still entrenched in the sands where she grounded. *Mauna Ala* was last seen in two large pieces with the bow pointed eastward toward shore and the stern parallel to the surf.

Any remaining wreckage of the steel hull is likely just offshore, in the surf zone. Parts of the wreck may be occasionally uncovered under the water in the sand, but any exposed areas would quickly get pounded by the powerful and destructive surf. Crabbers who have laid gear in this area for years indicate they have not found any obstructions, which adds to the likelihood that the wreck is beneath the surface of the sand.[3] Being in the surf zone, it is not a good candidate for a boat-based archaeological survey using divers or remote sensor equipment such as a magnetometer.

Objects in museums, such as a candy tin or name board, help bring the stories of the shipwreck to life and share the memories of the people who experienced the event, while archaeology seeks to scientifically document the physical remains in their original location. Together, along with oral histories and other primary source material found in archives, a more complete and accurate record of the historical event emerges.

The United States was still adjusting to the new state of war in December 1941 when *Mauna Ala* was stranded. The wreck provided a connection between the Oregon coast and the events of Pearl Harbor at a turning point in American history. The coast guard announced that navigational aids would be back in service on December 15 so other ships would not wreck while attempting to locate the mouth of the Columbia River.

A victim of the Graveyard of the Pacific, this freighter was one among thousands of wrecks along the Pacific Northwest coast. *Mauna Ala* was not able to deliver holiday supplies to the residents of Hawaii, but may have provided a welcome distraction for tense Oregonians in the early days of World War II. The remains of the broken ship are buried deep under the sand, perhaps forever, unless the ever-shifting coastline decides to reveal more of her story.

Robert Johnson

EPILOGUE

There are innumerable shipwrecks out there, and so many of them have fascinating legacies. It feels like we could spend a lifetime just researching the full lifecycle of a single ship. It is not just about the tragedies and the heroes, although the stories do help provide historical and cultural context as well as keep us entertained. We intentionally created this book in an informal style, accessible for everyone, rather than use the format of an archaeological report. One of the most important parts of our mission is to share research results, whether through our website, social media, lectures, or publications such as this book.

The Pacific Northwest coast has a lot to offer for anyone interested in maritime history. Artifacts people have picked up from shipwrecks, often from ships long gone but not forgotten, can be found at the local coastal museums. The Westport Maritime Museum has a display on *Trinidad*. The Columbia Pacific Heritage Museum in Ilwaco has items from *Iowa* and other shipwrecks. The Columbia River Maritime Museum has the two restored *Shark* cannons and exhibits about the Graveyard of the Pacific. The Nehalem Valley Historical Society in Manzanita is worth a visit for its Beeswax Wreck, *Glenesslin*, and *Mimi* displays. The Cannon Beach History Center and Museum, which has the third *Shark* cannon, the Tillamook Pioneer Museum, Garibaldi Museum, and others also have revolving displays on shipwrecks.

Remains of some shipwrecks themselves can be found at the coast as well. A boiler from a steam-powered schooner named *J Marhoffer*, which burned in 1910, can be seen during especially low tides in what is now aptly named Boiler Bay near Depot Bay, Oregon. *Emily Reed* and others sometimes make an appearance, when winter storms and tidal conditions are just right. The bow of *Peter Iredale* is always on display at Fort Stevens State Park.

Peter Iredale is the most photographed shipwreck on the Oregon coast today and a popular subject of #graveyardofthepacific on social media. The 287-foot British bark went aground on Clatsop Beach at 6:00 a.m. on October 25, 1906, in the area just south of the Columbia River. She was a four-masted iron and steel cargo ship sailing from Salina Cruz, Mexico, en route to Portland, Oregon, where she was to pick up a load of wheat for the UK. The ship reportedly was forced into the breakers by strong winds out of the north and a surging current while waiting for a pilot near the mouth of the river. The entire crew, plus two stowaways, were brought safely to shore with little drama. Much of the metal was salvaged during World War I. The bow

Peter Iredale *after wrecking in 1906.* **Courtesy of the Columbia River Maritime Museum, Astoria**

Peter Iredale *in May 2016.* ***Courtesy of the Maritime Archaeological Society. Photographer Jennifer Kozik***

is still visible today, facing north where the ship came to rest parallel to the shore. *Peter Iredale* has been a tourist attraction almost from the day she grounded. Occasionally, tides scrape away more of the sand to reveal well-preserved lower deck frames and part of a mast with its mast step.

It is interesting to ponder what makes a shipwreck important. Other than the fact that portions of the ships are still remaining today, *Peter Iredale* and *J Marhoffer* are considered fairly average. Some wrecks capture our imagination because they have harrowing stories of death and survival. Others provide a unique view into a particular aspect of our history. Some wrecks became places on maps: Peacock Spit, Desdemona Sands, Cannon Beach, Boiler Bay, Deadmans Cove. A few, like the Beeswax Wreck, are legendary because they have been a long-standing mystery for generations.

The sea and the coastline hold secrets, hidden just out of sight beneath the sand and waves, waiting to be discovered. It speaks to our souls somehow, providing a sense of connection to the world and its history, out there under the shiny waters. To quote F. Scott Fitzgerald, "So we beat on, boats against the current, borne back ceaselessly into the past." And so we will carry on, investigating historical shipwrecks wherever their stories take us.

ACKNOWLEDGMENTS

"It'd be cool if you didn't tell anyone where this trail is." A surfer disappeared into the shadows of the dense pines, ferns, and shrubs clinging to the cliff wall. It was a hidden, steep, narrow path with ropes up to the street, marked by the occasional upside-down empty Hershey's Chocolate Syrup bottle on a wooden stake. We followed. Our small research team was exhausted and hungry after a long day of hiking around the rugged terrain. "Already forgotten," we said. I have not forgotten the experience, though. It was like a quirky, magical, wooded fairyland. Thank you for the shortcut. Your secret location is safe with us.

Two of the most well-known and beloved authors of shipwreck history in the Pacific Northwest are James Gibbs and Don Marshall. The books written by these two authors have kept the memories of many shipwrecks alive in the public imagination. No literary work on shipwrecks of the Pacific Northwest should be started without first surveying their works. Some of our contributors were hooked on the stories of shipwrecks by these authors, igniting a lifelong passion to learn more about local shipwrecks. We are thankful for their legacies.

This book would not have been possible without the Columbia River Maritime Museum. We would like to send our thanks to all of the employees and volunteers at CRMM, including Executive Director Sam Johnson, Deputy Director Bruce Jones, Curator Jeff Smith, Collections Manager Matthew Palmgren, and Librarian Marcy Dunning.

The museum's Ted M. Natt Library provided research material and space for our faithful group of Maritime Archaeological Society volunteer researchers. The library furnished our investigators with unique imagery and one-of-a-kind ship documentation, including shipyard drawings and sketches. Our dedicated team meets weekly at the CRMM library. Thanks to our research team, including Tod Lundy, Carole Elder, Cameron Brister, Ellen Raabe, Randle and Jim Sharpe, Larry Thormahalen, Robert Johnson, and Mike Brown.

It is with enduring gratitude that we thank all of the MAS board members and advisers who helped get our organization up and running. Chris Dewey, Jeff Groth, Scott Williams, and Richard (Rick) Rogers have been involved with MAS from the beginning. It was the vision of our founder and president, Chris Dewey, that made this organization and this book a reality. Thank you also to Jerry Ostermiller, Mandi Anderson, Michelle Hannum, Charlie Beacham, Keith Seibel, and Bill Zanke for serving on our board at one time or another.

Scott S. Williams, principal investigator on the Beeswax Wreck Project, would like to extend a special thank-you to all of the volunteers who have helped with the BWP over the years. Field Director Christopher Dewey and Project Manager Rick Rogers have long been involved in the search. Thank you to all of the project researchers, support crew, and project team members, including Ed Von der Porten, Mitch Marken, David Chaffee, Carol Chaffee, Dave Wellman, Jack W. Peters, Craig Andes, and Jessica Lally.

Eb Giesecke, Northwest historian, was the individual most active in researching and advocating for recognition of the Beeswax Wreck at Nehalem, Oregon. His interest in the wreck started as a child on family trips to the Oregon coast, and he began actively investigating the site in the 1950s. He was an important part of the Beeswax Wreck Project until his passing, and it is much of his original research that continues to drive this project. His scholarship and companionship are sorely missed by the BWP team. Fair winds and calm seas to you, Eb.

We have been fortunate for the amount of support our little all-volunteer nonprofit has received during this process. A debt of gratitude is owed to the many organizations and individuals who helped us bring the project to life. John Shaw of the Westport South Beach Historical Society and Museum, where the collection of Coast Guardsman Hilman John Persson is housed, provided valuable information about *Trinidad* and kept us informed about the adventures of the wandering shipwreck. The Oregon Historical Society Research Library and museums up and down the coast, including the Cannon Beach History Center and Museum, were very helpful. Tom Mock, Mark Beach, and

Thomas Campbell at the Nehalem Valley Historical Society in Manzanita have been very helpful with *Santo Cristo de Burgos* and *Glenesslin*. Don Best and his family have lived near the wreck of *Emily Reed* for three generations. His knowledge and stories are greatly appreciated. A special thank-you to retired US Coast Guard Chief Boatswain's Mate Tim Stenz and Chief Machinery Technician David Marsters for answering our questions and providing sources about US Coast Guard traditions, ratings, rank structure, lore, and anecdotes. Thanks to Dave Barrett, Bill Zanke, and Jeff Groth for regularly letting MAS use their boats despite the costs, distance, and time involved.

As the editor, I would like to extend a thank-you to my friends, family, and colleagues who were so patient during this experience. Thanks to my husband, Stephen, for tolerating all of my missed dinners and late nights. I greatly appreciate Jeff Groth for the research assistance and for putting up with my never-ending shipwreck questions, as well as Rick Rogers for providing valuable feedback on the manuscript. Rick is a diver, pilot, fearless explorer, author of *Shipwrecks of Hawaii*, and the official historian for Hawaiian Airlines. My non-consanguineal cousin Kelly Mabin was wonderful too, providing an impartial perspective on the chapters. Thanks to Will Fife and Nubez Jordan for accompanying me on maritime adventures. And a special thanks to Joanne Rideout and Finn J. D. John for their many wonderful nautical-themed local episodes of *The Ship Report* and *Offbeat Oregon History* podcasts. They kept us entertained on our many research and documentation trips up and down the coast.

Finally, Winnifred Herrschaft was a historian, librarian, hilarious storyteller, and all-around fabulous, feisty nonagenarian. She passed away on May 31, 2019, before I could show her the finished manuscript for this book. *Slàinte mhath*, my dear Scotch-Canadian friend. I raise a drink in your name.

NOTES

Introduction

1. Dr. Dennis Griffin, personal email communication, February 2019. Many of those 140 are just a verification of location, with no formal site reports, according to the Oregon SHPO archaeologist.

Santo Cristo de Burgos

1. Samuel Cotton, *Stories of Nehalem* (Chicago: M. A. Donohue, 1915). Cotton provides an excellent overview of the beeswax and treasure stories and legends. Page 46 has the memorable line: "That a ship carrying much beeswax was wrecked here is without question. No story of the Nehalem country has ever been told without a reference to it and all these are substantiated by the immense quantity of wax found scattered along the beach." Cotton also has an excellent discussion of the natural mineral wax versus beeswax issue.

2. Scott S. Williams, "The Beeswax Wreck, a Manila Galleon in Oregon, USA," in *Early Navigation in the Asia-Pacific Region: A Maritime Archaeological Perspective,* ed. Chunming Wu (Singapore: Springer, 2016).

3. *Oregon Historical Quarterly* 119, no. 2 (Summer 2018). This special issue on the Beeswax Wreck summarizes the archaeological, historical, and archival information known about *Santo Cristo de Burgos* and why it is likely the wreck at Nehalem.

4. William L. Schurz, *The Manila Galleon* (New York: E. P. Dutton, 1939). Often considered "the Bible" of Manila galleon research, Schurz is a standard and indispensable reference, but there are some errors of fact, including his claim that *Santo Cristo de Burgos* burned in the western Pacific.

USS *Shark*

1. The "Sandwich Islands" was a British name put in place by Captain Cook in 1778. The name was used on maps for many years and was referred to as such in "Report of Lieutenant Neil M. Howison on Oregon, 1846." From its very first constitution in 1840, however, the island chain was called Hawaii. The name slowly caught on with foreign ships visiting in the 1840s, so the crew of *Shark* likely heard both terms in Honolulu during their repair and supply stop before heading for the Columbia River in 1846.

2. Newly elected president James K. Polk had campaigned on the idea of Manifest Destiny, spreading the US borders across the North American continent. *Shark* had been in Hawaii for repairs from sometime in April until June 23 under orders of Commodore Sloat, who led the Pacific Squadron in patrols between the Hawaiian Islands and Mazatlan. While the crew of *Shark* must have known tensions were high along the California coast and the southern border, it is not clear how much they knew about the war. While shipwrecked in the Northwest, Howison "heard overland of hostilities with Mexico" and "news of the Oregon treaty, Mexican war, and occupation of California" from *Toulon* when the bark returned from Hawaii, according to his report to the commander of the Pacific Squadron dated February 1, 1847.

Desdemona

1. Abernethy was recruited by Reverend Jason Lee in 1840 as part of the Methodist "Great Reinforcement." As governor, he made it his mission to make the sale and production of alcohol illegal. "We are in an Indian country; men will be found who will supply them with liquor as long as they have beaver, blankets, and horses to pay for it," he said in an 1846 speech to the state legislature. After he sold *Desdemona*, the ship often brought ale and porter to the territory.

2. There is another story from *Pacific Graveyard* by James Gibbs that remains part of the popular lore regarding a bet contributing to the wreck of *Desdemona*. If the ship arrived in Astoria before the new year, the owner of the ship would buy Captain Williams a new suit of

clothes. No other source was found to corroborate this story, however, so it was not included.

3. The Corps of Discovery stayed near Chinook Point, now a National Historic Landmark in Fort Columbia State Park, for ten days before heading across the river to winter at Fort Clatsop, where they hoped hunting would be more favorable. Clark described Chinook Point as "a point of rocks about 40 feet high, from the top of which hill Side is open and assend[s] with a Steep assent to the tops of the mountains, a Deep nitch and two Small Streams above the Point." They also climbed Cape Disappointment to get a better view of the Pacific Ocean after their long journey.

4. *Multnomah* was the first steamer on the upper Willamette River. The side-wheeler arrived at Oregon City from the East Coast in 1851 aboard a bark in three pieces for assembly. In the quick letter Captain Williams sent off after the wreck of the ship, he said, "I should write more, but the *Multnomah* being about to leave I have not time."

Great Republic

1. The names of the eleven drowned crew were First Officer H. Lennon, William Johnson, J. Conner, Thomas McAvoy, Samuel McMurray, Frank Scott, Albert Hilton, Charles Muretz, Frank Mallory, Charles Bird, and James McDermitt, according to *Lewis & Dryden's Marine History of the Pacific Northwest*.

2. James P. Delgado, Jerry L. Ostermiller, and Daniel J. Lenihan, Isabella *or* Great Republic? *Implications of a Resurvey of a Shipwreck Site Eighteen Years After Discovery* (College Station, TX: Institute of Nautical Archaeology, 2012).

Emily Reed

1. After local newspapers picked up the story, the crew of another ship, the steamer *Washington*, which had just arrived in Portland, reported they had seen what they believed was *Emily Reed* at about 2:00 a.m. on the night of the wreck. The sailing ship they saw was about five miles offshore and heading straight in, toward the coast. They said they were a

little too far away to communicate with the ship. A time-of-wreck news clipping (unsourced) titled "Captain and Wife, 2nd Mate and Three Seamen Safe" has an interesting story not seen elsewhere. The cook of the ship *Washington*, Robert Jones, had served on *Emily Reed* within the last year. He said the old ship was leaking so much on a voyage from Puget Sound to São Paulo that the crew was constantly at the pumps and there was knee-high water in the galley for much of the trip. "The truth of the matter is that she was about worn out on account of her age. Whenever she reached a port she had to be repaired," Jones is quoted as saying.

2. Several newspapers listed the first mate's surname as Dubie or Zuber rather than Zube, and there are several slight variations in spelling with the other crew members' names too. Ernest the cabin boy, a German, was spelled Ernst in some of the newspaper articles. Also, despite best efforts, the authors were unable to locate the first name of Mrs. Kessel.

3. Don Best, personal interview, June 2019. Don is full of stories about tracking and exploring the wreckage over the course of his life. As a child, he climbed into an air pocket underneath the exposed ribs with a flashlight and found a ship's whistle. He also tells a story of his grand-father taking a plank from the ship each year to burn on Christmas. The small copper nails that had held the copper sheeting burned magically, creating bright blue and green flames. Don still has one of those planks in his yard, which he shows to interested visitors.

Glenesslin

1. According to *The Last of the Windjammers*, there was an impression that those remaining on sailing ships were either older, stubborn traditionalists resistant to new technologies or young, ambitious men looking for sea time and fast promotions before transferring to jobs in the more desirable steamship fleet.

2. Captain Pritchard may have used the crimping practice as a way to swap out less qualified or less desirable crew members since it was becoming more difficult to find enough experienced sailors to handle the ship as successfully as in her glory days of record-holding fast voyages.

Portland and Seattle are also infamous for stories of another unscrupulous practice called shanghaiing. An unsuspecting sailor would supposedly wake up aboard a ship out to sea, after either passing out or getting knocked out in town. Stories of interconnected tunnels underneath local bars, brothels, and hotels where the unconscious men could be dropped or dragged are legendary. There is no known connection between *Glenesslin* and shanghaiing.

3. "A Follow Up Story on the Glenesslin Salvage" is an undated newspaper clipping that states, "Bert Gresham salvaged the two huge anchors by pulling them up the Neahkahnie Mountain face to the roadway with a donkey engine." There is a possibility that one of the anchors may have temporarily ended up in downtown Manzanita outside the post office where the San Dune Pub is located today. The photograph of the anchor is unsourced as well, however. While these are not primary sources, they may help spark the conversation about what happened to these items over the last century. The Nehalem Valley Historical Society is assisting with the search for what became of the anchors from *Glenesslin*.

Iowa

1. Captain Patch also reported that a distress call was heard by the Fort Stevens Radio Compass Station at 5:35 a.m., but other sources suggest there was only one distress call, around 4:00 a.m.

2. "List of Dead in Iowa Wreck," *Seattle Times*, January 13, 1936, p. 1. The names of the thirty-four officers and crew members who died aboard *Iowa* are: Edgar L. Yates, Carl C. Bendixen, Frank Caldwell, V. Cloherty, Theodore J. Frison, Charles Ogan, Elven Severine, Alfred G. Kreiger, Fred W. Whiteside, Donald D. Graham, Frank H. Hluick, James Houston, George Marr, Ed Cooper, William Tardy, Hubert Browne, Allan E. McCaughan, James M. McHenry, Tom E. Barrett, Edward F. Wolfsehr, Johannes Aben, Donald J. Kidd, Otto Doehring, Donald McLeon, Philip J. Nael, Wilbur W. Weltel, Edward Mislok, Milton A. K. Olsen, Walter Spencer, Homer T. Mercereau, Charles Steinmetz, James W. Welsh, August O. Meyers, and Marion J. Perich.

Trinidad

1. Numerous newspapers from the time of the wreck say there were twenty crew members rescued. The US Treasury Department Letter of Commendation from the Commandant to Boatswain Hilman J. Persson dated May 25, 1937, states twenty-one seamen were rescued, so that is the number used.

2. *Onondaga* is the same coast guard cutter that attempted to rescue the crew of SS *Iowa*. The United States Coast Guard was formed in 1915 by the merging of the U.S. Revenue Cutter Service, which was formed to enforce tariffs and prevent smuggling in 1790, and the U.S. Life-Saving Service, which had grown from an all-volunteer effort in the 1800s to save ships and crews in distress close to shore into an official Department of Treasury agency in 1878. The unofficial motto of the coast guard is "We have to go out but we don't have to come back."

Mauna Ala

1. Some secondary accounts suggest the ship did not know about the blackout. When the ship officers took the stand on December 12, they said they had expected the navigation lights at the mouth of the Columbia to be lighted. The Matson Navigation Company internal report said the ship knew about the blackout. Likely the crew knew about the blackout, but did not know how extensive it was.

2. It is not well documented whether the Christmas trees spilled immediately at the time of the stranding, but oral histories from veterans indicated that the trees were thought to be Japanese troops grounding on the night of the wreck.

3. Personal communication between local crabbers and lead project researcher, retired Columbia River Bar pilot Robert Johnson.

SOURCES

Books, Manuscripts, and Articles

Introduction

Griffin, Dennis. "A History of Underwater Archaeological Research in Oregon." *Journal of Northwest Anthropology* 47, no. 1 (Spring 2013).

Haglund, Michael E. *World's Most Dangerous: A History of the Columbia River Bar, Its Pilots and Their Equipment.* Astoria, OR: Columbia River Maritime Museum, 2011.

Lenihan, Daniel J. "Rethinking Shipwreck Archaeology." In *Shipwreck Anthropology*, edited by Richard A. Gould, 37–64. Albuquerque: University of New Mexico Press, 1983.

Muckelroy, Keith. *Maritime Archaeology.* New York: Cambridge University Press, 1978.

Stewart, David J. "Formation Processes Affecting Submerged Archaeological Sites: An Overview." *Geoarchaeology: An International Journal* 14, no. 6: 565–87.

Ward, A. I. K., P. Larcombe, and P. Veth. "A New Process-based Model for Wreck Site Formation." *Journal of Archaeological Science* 26, no. 5 (May 1999): 561–70.

Santo Cristo de Burgos

Atwater, Brian F., Satoko Musumi-Rokkaku, Kenji Satake, Yoshinobu Tsuji, Kazue Ueda, and David Yamaguchi. *The Orphan Tsunami of 1700: Japanese Clues to a Parent Earthquake in North America.* U.S. Geological Survey Professional Paper 1707. Seattle: University of Washington Press, 2005.

Blair, Emma Helen, and James A. Robertson. *The Philippine Islands, 1493–1803: Explorations by Early Navigators, Descriptions of the Islands and Their Peoples, Their History and Records of the Catholic Missions, as Related in Contemporaneous Books and Manuscripts,*

Showing the Political, Economic, Commercial and Religious Conditions of Those Islands from Their Earliest Relations with European Nations to the Beginning of the Nineteenth Century / Translated from the Originals. Cleveland, OH: A. H. Clark, 1903–1909.

Cook, Warren L. *Flood Tide of Empire.* New Haven and London: Yale University Press, 1973.

Cooper, William S. *Coastal Sand Dunes of Oregon and Washington.* Boulder, CO: Geological Society of America Memoir 72, 1958.

Cotton, Samuel. *Stories of Nehalem.* Chicago: M. A. Donohue, 1915.

Coues, Elliott. *New Light on the Early History of the Greater Northwest: The Manuscript Journals of Alexander Henry, Fur Trader of the Northwest Company, and of David Thompson, Official Geographer and Explorer of the Same Company, 1799–1814.* Vol. 2. New York: Francis P. Harper, 1897.

Dahlgren, Erik W. *Were the Hawaiian Islands visited by the Spaniards before their discovery by Captain Cook in 1778? A contribution to the geographical history of the North Pacific Ocean especially of the relations between America and Asia in the Spanish period.* 1917. Reprint, New York: AMS Press, 1977.

Davidson, George. *Pacific Coast. Coast Pilot of California, Oregon, and Washington Territory.* Washington, DC: Government Printing Office, 1869.

———. *Pacific Coast. Coast Pilot of California, Oregon, and Washington Territory.* Washington, DC: Government Printing Office, 1889.

Erlandson, Jon, Robert Losey, and Neil Peterson. "Early Maritime Contact on the Northern Oregon Coast: Some Notes on the 17th Century Nehalem Beeswax Ship." In *Changing Landscapes: "Telling Our Stories," Proceedings of the Fourth Annual Coquille Cultural Preservation Conference,* edited by Jason Younker, Mark A. Tveskov, and David G. Lewis. North Bend, WA: Coquille Indian Tribe, 2001.

Fish, Shirley. *The Manila-Acapulco Galleons: The Treasure Ships of the Pacific, with an Annotated List of the Transpacific Galleons 1565–1815.* Central Milton Keynes, UK: AuthorHouse, 2011.

Gibbs, George, William F. Tolmie, and Gregory Mengarini. *Tribes of Western Washington and Northwestern Oregon*. Seattle, WA: Shorey, 1970; facsimile reproduction, 2011. Extract from vol. 1 of *Contributions to American Ethnology*, Washington, DC, 1877.

Gibbs, James. *Disaster Log of Ships*. Seattle, WA: Superior, 1971.

Giesecke, Eb W. *Beeswax, Teak and Castaways: Searching for Oregon's Lost Protohistoric Asian Ship*. Manzanita, OR: Nehalem Valley Historical Society, 2007.

Hill, Percy. *Romance and Adventure in Old Manila*. Manila: Philippine Education Co., 1928.

———. *Romantic Episodes in Old Manila: Church and State in the Hands of a Merry Jester—Time*. Manila: Sugar News Press, 1925.

Hobson, John. "North Pacific Prehistoric Wrecks." *Oregon Native Son* 2, no. 5 (October 1900): 222–24.

Lally, Jessica. "Analysis of the Beeswax Shipwreck Porcelain Collection." In *Proceedings of the 2nd Asia-Pacific Regional Conference on Underwater Cultural Heritage*, edited by Hans Van Tilburg, Sila Tiripati, Veronica Walker Vadillo, Brian Fahy, and Jun Kimura. Honolulu: Electric Pencil, 2014.

———. "Analysis of the Chinese Blue and White Porcelain Associated with the Beeswax Wreck, Nehalem, Oregon." Master's thesis, Department of Anthropology, Central Washington University, 2008.

Lee, Daniel, and Joseph Frost. *Ten Years in Oregon*. Fairfield, WA: Ye Galleon Press, 1968.

Marshall, Don. *Oregon Shipwrecks*. Portland, OR: Binford & Mort, 1984.

Minto, John. "The Number and Condition of the Native Race in Oregon When First Seen by White Men." *Quarterly of the Oregon Historical Society* 1, no. 3 (September 1900): 298–315.

Oregon Historical Quarterly 119, no. 2 (Summer 2018). Special issue: *Oregon's Manila Galleon*.

Palmer, Joel. *Journal of Travels Over the Rocky Mountains, to the Columbia River; Made During the Years 1845 and 1846: Containing Minute*

Descriptions of the Valleys of the Willamette, Umpqua, and Clamet; a General Description of the Oregon Territory; Its Inhabitants, Climate, Soil, Productions, Etc., Etc.; a List of Necessary Outfits for Emigrants; and a table of Distances from Camp to Camp on the Route. Cincinnati, OH: J. A. & U. P. James, 1847.

Parker, Samuel. *Journal of an Exploring Tour Beyond the Rocky Mountains, Under the Direction of the A.B.C.F.M. Performed in the Years 1835, '36, and '37; Containing a Description of the Geography, Geology, Climate, and Production, and the Number, Manners, and Customs of the Natives.* Ithaca, NY: Mack, Andrus & Woodruff, 1838.

Peterson, Curt D., Scott S. Williams, Kenneth Cruikshank, and John Dubé. "Geoarchaeology of the Nehalem Spit: Redistribution of Beeswax Galleon Wreck Debris by Cascadia Earthquake and Tsunami (~A.D. 1700), Oregon, USA." *Geoarchaeology: An International Journal* 26, no. 2 (March/April 2011): 219–44.

Powell, Mary E. "The Legends of Nehalem." *Mazama* 6, no. 2 (December 1921): 59–63.

Rogers, Thomas. *Nehalem: A Story of the Pacific, A.D. 1700.* McMinnville, OR: H. L. Heath, 1898.

Scammon, Capt. C. M. "In and Around Astoria." *Overland Monthly* 3, no. 6 (December 1869): 495–99.

Scheans, Daniel, Thomas Churchill, Alison Stenger, and Yvonee Hajda. "Summary Report on the 1989 Excavations at the Cronin Point Site (35-TI-4B) Nehalem State Park, Oregon." Manuscript on file. Salem, OR: Oregon State Historic Preservation Office, 1990.

Schurz, William L. *The Manila Galleon.* New York: E. P. Dutton, 1959 (paperback edition). First published 1939.

Stafford, Orin F. "The Wax of Nehalem Beach." *Oregon Historical Quarterly* 9, no. 1 (March 1908).

Stenger, Allison. "Physical Evidence of Shipwrecks on the Oregon Coast in Prehistory." *CAHO: Current Archaeological Happenings in Oregon* 30, no. 1 (Spring 2005): 9–13.

Swan, James G. *The Northwest Coast; Or, Three Years' Residence in Washington Territory.* 6th ed. Seattle and London: University of

Washington Press, 1998. First published 1857 by Harper & Brothers (New York).

Victor, Frances Fuller. *All Over Oregon and Washington: Observations on the Country, Its Scenery, Soil, Climate, Resources, and Improvements, with an Outline of Its Early History, and Remarks on Its Geology, Botany, Mineralogy, etc.; Also, Hints to Immigrants and Travelers Concerning Routes, the Cost of Travel, the Price of Land, Etc.* San Francisco: John H. Carmany, 1872.

Williams, Scott S. "The Beeswax Wreck, a Manila Galleon in Oregon, USA." In *Early Navigation in the Asia-Pacific Region: A Maritime Archaeological Perspective,* edited by Chunming Wu. Singapore: Springer, 2016.

———. "Report on 2007 Fieldwork of the Beeswax Wreck Project, Nehalem Bay, Tillamook County, Oregon." Manuscript on file. Salem OR: Oregon State Parks and Oregon State Historic Preservation Office, 2008.

———. "A Research Design to Conduct Archaeological Investigations at the Site of the 'Beeswax Wreck' of Nehalem Bay, Tillamook County, Oregon." Prepared by the Beeswax Wreck Project. Manuscript on file. Salem, OR: Oregon State Parks and Oregon State Historic Preservation Office, 2007.

———. "Tsunami and Salvage: The Archaeological Landscape of the Beeswax Wreck, Oregon, USA." In *Formation Processes of Maritime Archaeological Landscapes and Sites,* edited by Alicia Caporaso. New York: Springer, 2017.

Woodward, John. "Prehistoric Shipwrecks on the Oregon Coast? Archaeological Evidence." In *Contributions to the Archaeology of Oregon 1983–1986,* edited by Kenneth Ames. Association of Oregon Archaeologists Occasional Papers No. 3, 1986.

Woodward, John, James White, and Ronald Cummings. "Paleoseismicity and the Archaeological Record: Areas of Investigation on the Northern Oregon Coast." *Oregon Geology* 25, no. 3 (May 1990).

USS *Shark*

Bajdek, Brennan P. "The Analysis and Conservation of Two 18-Pounder Carronades from the U.S. Navy Schooner *Shark*." Master's thesis, Texas A&M University, 2012.

Bauer, K. Jack, and Stephen S. Roberts. *Register of Ships of the U.S. Navy, 1775–1990: Major Combatants*. Westport, CT: Greenwood Press, 1991.

Canney, Donald L. *Sailing Warships of the US Navy*. Annapolis, MD: Naval Institute Press, 2001.

Chapelle, Howard Irving. *The History of the American Sailing Navy: The Ships and Their Development*. New York: W. W. Norton, 1949.

Commager, Henry. "England and Oregon Treaty of 1846." *Oregon Historical Quarterly* 28, no. 1 (March 1927): 18–38.

Dennon, Jim. *The Schooner Shark, Shark Rock, and Cannon Beach*. Seaside, OR: published by the author, 1988.

———. "The Schooner Shark's Cannon." *CUMTUX* 9, no. 3 (1989): 3–13.

Gibbs, James. *Shipwrecks of the Pacific Coast*. Portland, OR: Binford & Mort, 1957.

Griffin, Dennis. "Recovery of Arch Cape Cannon: Report to the Oregon Parks and Recreation Department and the Department of State Lands Regarding the Discovery of Two Cannon at Arch Cape." Salem OR: Oregon State Historic Preservation Office, 2008.

Himes, George H. "Letters by Burr Osborn, Survivor of Howison Expedition to Oregon, 1846." *Oregon Historical Quarterly* 14, no. 4 (December 1913): 355–65.

Howerton, Norman A. "The U.S. Schooner Shark." *Oregon Historical Quarterly* 40, no. 3 (September 1939): 288–91. http://www.jstor.org/stable/20611200.

Howison, Neil M. *Lieut. Neil M. Howison, United States Navy, To the Commander of the Pacific Squadron; Being the Result of the Examination in the Year 1846 of the Coast, Harbors, Rivers, Soil, Productions,*

Climate, and Population of the Territory of Oregon. Washington, DC: U.S. House of Representatives, 1846.

———. "Report of Lieutenant Neil M. Howison on Oregon, 1846: A Reprint." *Quarterly of the Oregon Historical Society* 14, no. 1 (March 1913): 1–60. https://www.jstor.org/stable/20609921.

Jampoler, Andrew C. A. "Slavery and the U.S. Navy's Africa Squadron." *Naval History* 33, no.1 (February 2019): 40–45.

Marshall, Don. *Oregon Shipwrecks.* Portland, OR: Binford & Mort, 1984.

Mooney, James L., ed. *The Dictionary of American Naval Fighting Ships.* Washington, DC: U.S. Government Printing Office, 1976.

Shine, Gregory Paynter. "'A Gallant Little Schooner': The U.S. Schooner Shark and the Oregon Country, 1846." *Oregon Historical Quarterly* 109, no. 4 (Winter 2008): 536–65.

Desdemona

Abernethy, George. Papers, 1836–1897. Oregon Historical Society, Portland, OR.

Desdemona Donor and Accession Records. Columbia River Maritime Museum, Astoria, OR.

"The Entire Bark of The Desdemona." Oregon Imprints Collection, 1845–1870. Oregon Historical Society, Portland, OR.

Fairburn, William Armstrong. *Merchant Sail.* Center Lovell, ME: Fairburn Marine Educational Foundation, 1945–55.

Gibbs, James A. *Pacific Graveyard.* Portland, OR: Binford & Mort, 1950.

Marshall, Don. *Oregon Shipwrecks.* Portland, OR: Binford & Mort, 1984.

McArthur, Lewis A. "Earliest Oregon Post Offices as Recorded at Washington." *Oregon Historical Quarterly* 41, no. 1 (March 1940): 53–71.

Pope, Seth Luen. Papers, 1710–1979. "Log of the *Desdemona* from Oak Point on the Columbia River to San Francisco 1855–1856."

SOURCES **155**

Diary (old vol. 8) 1856, Diary (old vol. 9) 1857. Oregon Historical Society, Portland, OR.

Rasmussen, Louis J. *San Francisco Ship Passenger Lists.* Vol. 3: November 7, 1851, to June 17, 1852. Provo, UT: Clearfield, 2003.

State of Washington v. State of Oregon. Transcript of Record, Supreme Court of the United States, 1906.

Turnbull, George S. *History of Oregon Newspapers.* Portland, OR: Binford & Mort, 1939.

Wright, E. W. *Lewis & Dryden's Marine History of the Pacific Northwest: An Illustrated Review of the Growth and Development of the Maritime Industry, from the Advent of the Earliest Navigators to the Present Time, with Sketches and Portraits of a Number of Well Known Marine Men.* 6th ed. New York: Antiquarian Press, 1961.

Great Republic

Campbell, J. F. *My circular notes: extracts from journals, letters sent home, geological and other notes, written while travelling westwards round the world, from July 6, 1874, to July 6, 1875.* London: Macmillan, 1876.

Delgado, James P., Jerry L. Ostermiller, and Daniel J. Lenihan. Isabella *or Great Republic? Implications of a Resurvey of a Shipwreck Site Eighteen Years After Discovery.* College Station, TX: Institute of Nautical Archaeology, 2012.

Gibbs, James A. *Pacific Graveyard.* Portland, OR: Binford & Mort, 1950.

Kemble, John Haskell. *Side-Wheelers Across the Pacific.* San Francisco: San Francisco Museum of Science and Industry, 1942.

Ostermiller, Jerry. *Reconnaissance Survey Report: Shipwreck Isabella, 29 June 1994.* Astoria, OR: Columbia River Maritime Museum, 1994.

Roberts, Andrew P. "*Great Republic*: A Historical and Archaeological Analysis of a Pacific Mail Steamship." Master's thesis, Department of Anthropology, Texas A&M University, 2008.

White, James Seeley. "Mapping the Isabella Shipwreck." In Lang, MA (ed). Coldwater Diving for Science...1987. Proceedings of the

American Academy of Underwater Sciences annual scientific diving symposium 31 October - 1 November 1987, Seattle, Washington, USA, 1987.

Wright, E. W. *Lewis & Dryden's Marine History of the Pacific Northwest: An Illustrated Review of the Growth and Development of the Maritime Industry, from the Advent of the Earliest Navigators to the Present Time, with Sketches and Portraits of a Number of Well Known Marine Men.* 6th ed. New York: Antiquarian Press, 1961.

Emily Reed

Aherns, Corrie, Jessica Byers, and John G. Jones. "The Use of Pollen Analysis in the Determination of Coal Origin: Implications for the Identification of an Oregon Shipwreck." Washington State University, Pullman. Poster presented at the 61st Annual Northwest Anthropology Conference, Victoria, BC, 2008.

Biscoe, Mark W. *Merchant of the Medomak: Stories from Waldoboro Maine's Golden Years 1860–1910.* Newcastle, ME: Waldoboro Historical Society, 2004.

Griffin, Dennis. "A History of Underwater Archaeological Research in Oregon." *Journal of Northwest Anthropology* 47, no. 1 (Spring 2013): 1–24.

Lloyd's Register of British and Foreign Shipping. London: Cox and Wyman, printers, 1897.

Marshall, Don. *Oregon Shipwrecks.* Portland, OR: Binford & Mort, 1984.

McCarthy, Michael. *Ships' Fastenings: From Sewn Boat to Steamship.* College Station: Texas A&M University Press, 2005.

Milne, Gustav, Colin McKewan, and Damien Goodburn. *Nautical Archaeology on the Foreshore: Hulk Recording on the Medway.* London: Royal Commission on the Historical Monuments of England, 1998.

Glenesslin

Bladen, Vincent W. *An Introduction to Political Economy.* London: Humphrey Milford, Oxford University Press, 1941.

Buhle, Paul, and Edward Rice-Maximin. *William Appleman Williams: The Tragedy of Empire.* New York and London: Routledge, 1995.

Cohn, Raymond L. "The Transition from Sail to Steam in Immigration to the United States." *Journal of Economic History* 65, no. 2 (June 2005): 469–95. www.jstor.org/stable/3875069.

Gibbs, James. *Shipwrecks of the Pacific Coast.* Portland, OR: Binford & Mort, 1957.

Graham, Gerald S. "The Ascendancy of the Sailing Ship 1850–85." *Economic History Review* 9, no. 1 (1956): 74–88. www.jstor.org/stable/2591532.

Jacobs, Elizabeth Derr, and William R. Seaburg. *The Nehalem Tillamook: An Ethnography.* Corvallis: Oregon State University Press, 2003.

Jones, Gerald Norman. "Interlude in Steam." *Bulletin* (Liverpool Nautical Research Society) 42, no. 1 (Summer 1998): 7.

———. "Papers of Commodore Gerald Norman Jones CBE, DSO." Administrative/Biographical History, 1902–1960. Archifau Ynys Môn / Anglesey Archives, Llangefni, Wales.

Lloyd's Register of British and Foreign Shipping. London: Cox and Wyman, printers, 1898, 1905.

Lubbock, Basil. *The Last of the Windjammers.* Boston: Charles E. Lauriat, 1927.

McCarthy, Michael. *Ships' Fastenings: From Sewn Boat to Steamship.* College Station: Texas A&M University Press, 2005.

Muckelroy, Keith. *Maritime Archaeology.* New York: Cambridge University Press, 1978.

"No. 7617 Glenesslin." Findings and Order of a Naval Court Held at the British Consulate in Portland, Oregon. MSS 1983.181.2. Columbia River Maritime Museum, Astoria, OR.

Pearson, Clara, Elizabeth Derr Jacobs, and Melville Jacobs. *Nehalem Tillamook Tales.* Eugene: University of Oregon Books, 1959.

Williams, William Appleman. "Notes on the Death of a Ship and the End of a World: The Grounding of the British Bark Glenesslin at Neahkahnie Mountain on 1 October 1913." *American Neptune* 41, no. 1 (January 1981): 122–38.

Iowa

Alt, David, and Donald Hyndman. *Northwest Exposures: A Geologic Story of the Northwest*. Missoula, MT: Mountain Press, 1995.

American Maritime Cases. Vol. 2. Published under the auspices of the Maritime Law Association of the United States, 1936.

Cox, Ross. *The Columbia River*. Norman: University of Oklahoma Press, 1957.

Executive Order 549, Prescribing Official Manner of Designating Vessels of the United States Navy. Signed by President Theodore Roosevelt, January 8, 1917.

Freeman, Otis, and Howard Martin. *The Pacific Northwest*. New York: John Wiley and Sons, 1942.

Gibbs, James. *Pacific Graveyard*. Portland, OR: Binford & Mort, 1993.

Grandin, Greg. *Fordlandia: The Rise and Fall of Henry Ford's Forgotten Jungle City*. New York: Metropolitan Books, 2009.

Haglund, Michael. *World's Most Dangerous: A History of the Columbia River Bar, Its Pilots and Their Equipment*. Astoria, OR: Columbia River Maritime Museum, 2011.

ICF International, Southeastern Archaeological Research, and Davis Geoarchaeological Research. *Inventory and Analysis of Coastal and Submerged Archaeological Site Occurrence on the Pacific Outer Continental Shelf*. Report prepared for the U.S. Department of the Interior, Bureau of Ocean Energy Management, Pacific OCS Region, dated November 2013.

Launer, Donald. *Dictionary of Nautical Acronyms and Abbreviations*. Dobbs Ferry, NY: Sheridan House, 2006.

List of Merchant Vessels of the United States 1920. Washington, DC: Government Printing Office, 1920.

Miller, Emma. *Clatsop County, Oregon: A History*. Portland, OR: Binford & Mort, 1958.

Munro, Sarah Baker. "The Seventy-Fifth Anniversary of the New Deal: Oregon's Legacy." *Oregon Historical Quarterly* 109, no. 2 (Summer 2008): 304–11.

Pollard, Lancaster. *History of the State of Washington*. Portland, OR: Binford & Mort, 1941.

Record of American and Foreign Shipping. New York: American Bureau of Shipping, American Lloyd's, 1920.

Register of Ships Owned by United States Shipping Board. Washington, DC: Government Printing Office, 1920.

Richardson Associates, and United States. *Master Plan for Columbia River at the Mouth: Oregon and Washington*. Seattle: Richardson Associates, 1976.

Schwantes, Carlos. *Columbia River: Gateway to the West*. Moscow, ID: University of Idaho Press, 2000.

United States Department of Commerce, Bureau of Marine Inspection and Navigation. *Merchant Vessels of the United States*. Washington, DC: Government Printing Office, 1936.

United States Department of Labor. *Monthly Labor Review* 45, July to December 1937. Washington, DC: Government Printing Office, 1939.

Willis, Samuel, Bradley Bowen, Emily Ragsdale, and Jennifer Olander. *Cultural Resources Survey for the Wallacut-Baker Bay Property*. Columbia Land Trust Estuarine Habitat Restoration Project, Pacific County, Washington. Portland, OR: Historical Research Associates, 2013.

Trinidad

"Boatswain's Mate NAVEDTRA 14343A." US Navy Center for Surface Combat Systems, 2010.

Galluzzo, John J. "'Those Guys Got Plenty of Guts, Take It from Me': Hilman J. Persson and the Rescue of the Crew of the Trinidad." *Wreck & Rescue* 17 (Fall 2001): 14–17.

Gibbs, James A. *Pacific Graveyard*. Portland, OR: Binford & Mort, 1950.

Lewis, Dana. "U.S. Coast Guard Enlisted Ratings Specialty Marks & Distinguishing Marks 1915–2015; Warrant Officer & Chief Warrant Officer Specialty Devices 1898–2016." Coast Guard Historian's Office, December 2016.

"List of Regular and Reserve Commissioned and Warrant Officers on Active Duty in Order of Precedence and Temporary Members of the Reserve NAVCG 111." United States Coast Guard, June 30, 1944.

Lyman, John. "Pacific Coast Wooden Steam Schooners 1884–1924." *Marine Digest*, April 3, 1943–December 25, 1943.

McCarthy, Michael. *Ships' Fastenings: From Sewn Boat to Steamship*. College Station: Texas A&M University Press, 2005.

Persson, Hilman J. Papers. US Treasury Department Letter; Subject: Commendation. May 25, 1937. Westport Maritime Museum, Westport, WA.

Peterson, John R Jr. Hand-drawn map. "Ship Wreck Chart of Willapa Bay & Vicinity." Westport South Beach Historical Society archives.

Mauna Ala

Cressman, Robert J. *The Official Chronology of the U.S. Navy in World War II*. Annapolis, MD: US Naval Institute Press, 1999.

Gibbs, James A. *Pacific Graveyard*. Portland OR: Binford & Mort, 1950.

Haglund, Michael E. *World's Most Dangerous: A History of the Columbia River Bar, Its Pilots and Their Equipment*. Astoria, OR: Columbia River Maritime Museum, 2011.

Hickson, R. E., and F. W. Rodolf. "History of Columbia River Jetties." *Coastal Engineering Proceedings* 1 (1950): 283–398.

Kaminsky, George M., Peter Ruggiero, Maarten Buijsman, Diana McCandless, and Guy Gelfenbaum. "Historical Evolution of the Columbia River Littoral Cell." *Marine Geology* 273, nos. 1–4 (August 2010): 96–126.

Marshall, Don. *Oregon Shipwrecks*. Portland OR: Binford & Mort, 1984.

"Matson Navigation Company Loss of the S/S 'Mauna Ala' 10 December 1941." Unpublished Matson Navigation Company Internal Report.

Mauna Ala Donor and Accession Records. Columbia River Maritime Museum, Astoria, OR.

Mauna Ala Vessel File. Untitled personal letters. Columbia River Maritime Museum, Astoria, OR.

Stint, Fred A. *Matson Century of Ships*. Modesto, CA: privately published, 1982.

Epilogue

Gibbs, James. *Shipwrecks of the Pacific Coast*. Portland, OR: Binford & Mort, 1957.

Lloyd's Register of British and Foreign Shipping. London: Cox and Wyman, printers, 1898.

Marshall, Don. *Oregon Shipwrecks*. Portland, OR: Binford & Mort, 1984.

Spectre, Peter H., Willits Dyer Ansel, Paul Lipke, and Benjamin A. G. Fuller. *Boats: A Manual for Their Documentation*. Nashville, TN: American Association for State and Local History, 1993.

Newspapers and Online Resources

Introduction

Oregon State Marine Board. "Columbia River Bar Hazards." Accessed February 14, 2019. https://www.oregon.gov/osmb/forms-library/Documents/Publications/ColumbiaBar.pdf.

Santo Cristo de Burgos

McMinnville (OR) Telephone-Register. "Beeswax Ship Is Found." September 21, 1899.

Williams, Scott S. "A Manila Galleon in Oregon: Results of the 'Bees-wax Wreck' Research Project." In *Proceedings of the 2014 Asia-Pacific Regional Conference on Underwater Cultural Heritage.* Museum of Underwater Archaeology, May 2014. http://www.themua.org/collections/collections/show/1609.

USS *Shark*

Clement, Russell. "From Cook to the 1840 Constitution: The Name Change from Sandwich to Hawaiian Islands." *Hawaiian Journal of History* 14 (1980). http://hdl.handle.net/10524/495.

Crombie, Noelle. "Pair of Cannons Found on Oregon Coast Could Be from 1846 Ship." Oregonian/OregonLive, February 20, 2008. http://blog.oregonlive.com/breakingnews/2008/02/_the_discovery_of_a.html.

Johnson, Charles K. "Oregon Beach Bill." *The Oregon Encyclopedia.* Last updated April 15, 2019. https://oregonencyclopedia.org/articles/oregon_beach_bill/#.XNBNVpNKh0s.

Oregon Parks and Recreation Department. "Arch Cape Cannon Archaeology Report." Accessed June 15, 2019. https://www.oregon.gov/oprd/PARKS/pages/cannon_report.aspx.

US Department of the Navy, Naval History and Heritage Command. "Sunken Military Craft Act." Accessed June 15, 2019. https://www.history.navy.mil/content/dam/nhhc/research/underwater-archaeology/outreachmaterials/SMCA%20Brochure%202014.pdf.

Desdemona

Daily Alta California (San Francisco). Advertisements, column 2, September 20, 1855.

———. "From our Evening Edition Yesterday. Later from the Northern Coast: Arrival of Steamer Columbia." January 15, 1857.

———. Importations, September 11, 1852.

———. "Letter from Oregon." February 9, 1857.

———. "Loss of the Barque Desdemona." January 15, 1857.

del Mar, David Peterson. "George Abernethy (1807–1877)." *The Oregon Encyclopedia*. Last updated March 17, 2008. https://oregonencyclopedia.org/articles/abernethy_george_1807_1877_/#. XU8ZT3dFw2w.

"Good News from Home." The music of this song can be obtained at the store of George P. Reed, Boston. Monographic. Online text https://www.loc.gov/item/amss.as104710.

"Governor George Abernethy Administration July 14, 1845 to March 3, 1849: Legislative Messages." Oregon State Archives, Oregon Provisional and Territorial Records, 1845. Accessed August 31, 2019. https://sos.oregon.gov/archives/Pages/records/governors_guides.aspx

Hanable, William S. "Lighthouses on Cape Disappointment." History Link.org Essay 5622. Posted December 6, 2003. https://www.historylink.org/File/5622.

Historical Map & Chart Collection, US Department of Commerce, National Oceanic and Atmospheric Administration, Office of Coast Survey. "Reconnaissance of the Western Coast of the United States from Umpquah River to the Boundary, 1855." Accessed February 14, 2019. https://historicalcharts.noaa.gov.

National Park Service. "Lewis and Clark: Survey of Historic Sites and Buildings. Chinook Point Campsite Washington." Accessed August 31, 2019. https://www.nps.gov/parkhistory/online_books/lewisandclark/site40.htm

"National Register of Historic Places Inventory—Nomination Form" for Cape Disappointment Historic District, dated November 1, 1974. Received June 13, 1975; entered August 15, 1975. https://npgallery.nps.gov/GetAsset/3659575e-e6e0-4803-9b46 -5a79e98be69e.

Oregonian (Portland, OR). "Loss of the Bark Desdemona at Mouth of Columbia." January 13, 1857.

"Remnant of the Official Log of the Columbia." In *Voyages of the Columbia to the Northwest Coast: 1787–1790 and 1790–1793*, edited by Frederic W. Howay, 435–38. Boston: Massachusetts Historical Society, 1941. http://www.washington.edu/uwired/outreach.

Great Republic

"The Chinese Exclusion Act." Primary Documents in American History, Library of Congress. Accessed June 15, 2019. https://www.loc.gov/rr/program/bib/ourdocs/chinese.html.

Daily Alta California (San Francisco). "The Great Republic." August 6, 1867.

Earle, Rob. "Helm Commands." *The Misunderstood Mariner* (blog), August 24, 2011. http://misunderstoodmariner.blogspot.com/2011/08/helm-commands.html.

Lee, Douglas. "Chinese Americans in Oregon." *The Oregon Encyclopedia.* Last updated July 10, 2018. https://oregonencyclopedia.org/articles/chinese_americans_in_oregon/#.XOze61NKh0t.

New York Times. "The Great Republic: Launch of the Great Republic—China Line." November 10, 1866.

Wells, Robert. "Hidden Beneath the Ever-Changing Waters at the Mouth of the Columbia River." *Oregonian*, November 17, 2012.

Emily Reed

"Lewis and Clark at the Pacific: A Guide to the Lewis and Clark National and State Historical Parks." Cannon Beach, OR: Pelican Productions, 2006. https://www.nps.gov/lewi/planyourvisit/upload/parkguide06lr.pdf.

Morning Astorian (Astoria, OR). "Emily Reed Survivors." February 18, 1908.

———. "Emily Reed Wrecked." February 15, 1908.

———. "Survivors of Emily Reed." February 21, 1908.

———. "Waterfront Items." February 12, 1908.

Oregon Daily Journal (Portland, OR). "Complete Story of Lost Ship Told for First Time." March 1, 1908.

———. "Last of the Ship Emily Reed." February 19, 1908.

———. "Marine Intelligence: Coal Ships En Route." September 12,
    1907.
Pacific Commercial Advertiser (Honolulu). July 5, 1901.
Tobias, Lori. "Shifting Sands Reveal 102-Year-Old Shipwreck off
    Rockaway Beach." *Oregonian/OregonLive*, December 29, 2010.
    https://www.oregonlive.com/pacific-northwest-news/index
    .ssf/2010/12/shifting_sands_reveal_102-year-old_shipwreck_off_
    rockaway_beach.html.
The York Daily. "Wrecked Sailors Bring Body Home." February 19,
    1908.

Glenesslin

"Attributes Loss of Ship to His Mates." *Weekly Commercial News* 47, no.
    18 (November 1, 1913): 5.
Canright, Stephen Park. "Triple-Expansion Steam Engine Model." San
    Francisco Maritime Museum. Last updated March 1, 2015. https://
    www.nps.gov/safr/learn/historyculture/steamenginemodel.htm.
Engeman, Richard. "Shanghaiing in Portland and the Shanghai Tun-
    nels Myth." *The Oregon Encyclopedia.* Last updated March 17, 2018.
    https://oregonencyclopedia.org/articles/shanghai_tunnels_myth.
La Follette, Cameron, and Douglas Deur. "Neahkahnie Mountain."
    The Oregon Encyclopedia. Last updated May 8, 2019. https://oregon
    encyclopedia.org/articles/neahkahnie_mountain.
Morning Oregonian (Portland, OR). "Glenesslin Brings $560." Octo-
    ber 8, 1913.
———. "Ship Hits Rocks; All Aboard Safe." October 2, 1913.
Nehalem Bay (OR) Fishrapper. Untitled photo; caption reads in part,
    "Mayer photograph owned by Ray Norris of Nehalem shows the
    salvage operation going on October 17th with still yards of sail and
    lines to be salvaged." October 27, 1977.
North Wales Express (Caernarfon, Wales). "Death of a Carnarvon Lady
    Abroad." June 5, 1903.
———. "Marriage of Captain Barlow-Pritchard." November 2, 1900.

North Wales Observer and Express (Caernarfon, Wales). "The Ship 'Glenesslin' Two Record Passages." June 17, 1892.

Oregon Daily Journal (Portland, OR). "Captain Is Guilty of Negligence, in Wreck of Vessel." October 13, 1913.

———. "Only Investigation Will Determine Why Glenesslin Wrecked." October 2, 1913.

———. "Who Wants to Buy a Fairly Good Ship?" October 5, 1913.

San Francisco Call. "Grain Vessels Break Blockade, Six of the Fleet Will Race from Here to England." September 27, 1901.

———. "Has Been Many Times in Peril Glenesslin, Now in Port, Was Scuttled in New York." January 13, 1897.

———. "Her Cargo on Fire: Fierce Blaze on the Iron Ship Glenesslin." September 24, 1894.

San Francisco Chronicle. "Captain Drinks on Day of Wreck: Mates and Steward Shed New Light on Loss of British Ship Glenesslin." October 10, 1913.

Sunday Oregonian (Portland, OR). "Wreck of the Glenesslin at Necarney Mountain." October 13, 1913.

"Wreck of British Ship Glenesslin." Review of Marine Insurance and Shipping Law. *Railway and Marine News* 11 (1913): 30.

Iowa

Ancestry.com. *1930 Census of Merchant Seamen.* Provo, UT: Ancestry .com Operations, 2015. https://www.ancestry.com/search/collec tions/1930merchant.

Burns, Mac. "The Civilian Conservation Corps in Clatsop County." *Daily Astorian* (Astoria, OR), February 5, 2015.

Daily Astorian (Astoria, OR). "Coast Guard Plans Inquiry in Shipwreck." January 16, 1936.

———. "Columbia River Bar Improvement." May 10, 1881.

———. "Iowa's Wreck to Be Probed Martin Told." January 20, 1936.

———. "Laborite Asks Quiz of Wreck." January 15, 1936.

———. "None Survive in Worst Disaster Since Rosencrans." January 13, 1936.

———. "Sea Still Hides 28 Iowa Men." January 14, 1936.

———. "Wreck Sidelights." January 13, 1936.

Evening Star (Washington, DC). "34 Die as Storm Smashes Vessel." January 13, 1936.

Helena (MT) Independent. "All Aboard Big Vessel Feared Lost: Bodies Seen." January 13, 1936.

McClary, Daryl. "SS *Iowa* Wrecks on Peacock Spit at Cape Disappointment with a Loss of 34 Lives on January 12, 1936." HistoryLink.org Essay 11007. Posted February 20, 2015. http://www.historylink.org/File/11007.

Morning Oregonian (Portland, OR). "Pacific Coast Shipping Notes." December 29, 1929; September 20, 1920; and February 18, 1920.

"Register of Ships Owned by United States Shipping Board, August 1, 1920." Accessed September 1, 2019. http://www.shipscribe.com/shiprefs/USSB_1920/plans.html.

United States Department of Commerce, National Oceanic and Atmospheric Administration, Office of Coast Survey. "Hydrographic Survey Equipment." Accessed February 14, 2019. https://nauticalcharts.noaa.gov/learn/hydrographic-survey-equipment.html.

Seattle Times. "List of Dead in Iowa Wreck." January 13, 1936.

Shipbuilding History. "Western Pipe & Steel Co., South San Francisco and San Pedro CA (formerly Shaw-Batcher Company Ship Works [1917–1920] and including Southwestern Shipbuilding [1918–1922])." Last updated January 20, 2014. http://shipbuildinghistory.com/shipyards/large/westernpipe.htm.

Trinidad

Aberdeen (WA) Daily World. "Dangerous 1937 Willapa Shipwreck Rescue Recalled." August 4, 1955.

Aue, Barb. "Wandering Wreck of Washaway Makes Another Move." *South Beach Bulletin* (Westport WA), February 16, 2017. http://www.southbeachbulletin.com/news/wandering-wreck-of-washaway-makes-another-move.

Centralia (IL) Sentinel. "Hindenburg's Death Toll at Thirty-Five; Order Naval Inquiry." May 8, 1937.

———. "21 Men Rescued, One Is Missing as Vessel Sinks." May 8, 1937.

Chinook Observer (Long Beach, WA). "Vanishing Beach Reveals Mystery Shipwreck." January 11, 2010. https://www.chinookobserver .com/news/vanishing-beach-reveals-mystery-shipwreck/article_ eb689b72-3029-5182-87fa-02c23f51a37a.html.

High Point (NC) Enterprise. "One Lost When Ship Founders." May 8, 1937.

———. "Zeppelin Crash Death Toll Now 35." May 8, 1937.

Office of Coast Survey. United States Coast Pilot. Volume 7. NOAA National Centers for Environmental Information, 1934. https:// historicalcharts.noaa.gov/publications_cp.

Park, Kathy, and Tonya Bauer. "'Washaway Beach,' Fastest-Eroding Place on the West Coast, Cobbles Together a Solution." *NBC News,* November 24, 2018. https://www.nbcnews.com/news/us-news/washaway-beach-fastest-eroding-place-west-coast-cobbles-together-solution-n930646.

Reclamation Administration. "Maritime Deconstruction: Historic Large-Dimension Ocean Salvage Timbers." February 13, 2014. https://www.reclamationadministration.com/2014/02/13/ historic-large-dimension-ocean-salvage-timbers.

San Francisco Examiner. "One Drowned as S.F. Ship Piles on Beach." May 9, 1937.

———. "Prey of Gale." May 10, 1937.

———. "Wreckage of Trinidad Lines Willapa Beach." May 10, 1937.

Shipbuilding History. "Bendixsen Shipbuilding, Fairhaven CA." Last updated January 11, 2017. http://shipbuildinghistory.com/ship yards/19thcentury/bendixsen.htm.

Times (London). "Casualty Reports." May 11, 1937.

Mauna Ala

Astorian-Budget (Astoria, OR). "Hearing on Mauna Ala's Wreck Likely." December 14, 1941.

———. "Matson Freighter Beached Near Peter Iredale Wreck." December 11, 1941.

———. "Mauna Ala Sees Flash Signal Before Crashing." December 13, 1941.

———. "Ship Ashore on Clatsop Beach," December 12, 1941.

Honolulu Advisor. "New Solemnity Marks Xmas." December 25, 1941.

Honolulu Star-Bulletin. "Christmas Trees Reach Honolulu." December 12, 1941.

———. "First Christmas Trees." December 12, 1940.

———. "Newsprint Supply Cut by Mishap." December 12, 1941.

Matson, Inc. "History." Accessed August 26, 2018. https://www.matson .com/corporate/about_us/history.html.

McClary, Daryl C. "Fire Severely Damages Union Pacific Dock on Seattle Waterfront on July 17, 1929." HistoryLink.org Essay 10095. Posted June 18, 2012. http://historylink.org/File/10095.

"New Donation Highlights." Front Lines: The Oregon Military Museum Monthly Report. Clackamas, OR: 2012. Accessed June 15, 2019. http://oregonmilitarymuseum.org.

Oregon Parks and Recreation Department. "Fort Stevens State Park." Accessed June 15, 2019. https://oregonstateparks.org/index .cfm?do=parkPage.dsp_parkPage&parkId=129.

Rothman, Lily. "See Colorized Photos of a Peaceful Pearl Harbor in the Months Before War. *Life*, December 5, 2016. http://time .com/4567884/colorized-photos-pearl-harbor.

"The SS Mauna Ala." Blog. Cannon Beach History Center and Museum, May 29, 2015. Accessed September 1, 2019. https:// cbhistory.org/blog/articles/the-ss-mauna-ala/.

"US Navy." *Life*, October 28, 1940.

Epilogue

Allen, Cain. "The Wreck of the Peter Iredale." The Oregon History Project: A Project of the Oregon Historical Society. 2016; updated March 17, 2018. https://oregonhistoryproject.org/articles/historical-records/the-wreck-of-the-peter-iredale.

LIST OF CONTRIBUTORS

Editor and Contributor
Desdemona, Glenesslin: Jennifer Kozik earned a BA in Anthropology from the University of Missouri. She works in the stop-motion film industry by day and is a volunteer researcher, grant writer, and general devotee of all things maritime. Jennifer previously served for six years as Collections and Exhibits Manager and Public Programs Manager for the Washington County Museum in Oregon.

Contributors
Santo Cristo de Burgos: Scott Williams is a Cultural Resources Program Manager for the Washington State Department of Transportation. He has a master's degree in Anthropology from Washington State University and is a member of the Register of Professional Archaeologists. He has conducted fieldwork throughout the Pacific Northwest, Hawaii, the Marianas Islands, and Australia and has authored fourteen peer-reviewed articles, including four book chapters.

Shark: Jeff Smith is Senior Curator at the Columbia River Maritime Museum. Through the Scholars Program, Jeff earned his BA in History from Portland State University and some years later a Secondary Teaching Certificate in Education from Southern Oregon University. After a brief stint as an educator, he has held a collections stewardship role in the museum field for over thirty years and is the author of *Images of America: Astoria.*

Great Republic: Christopher Dewey is a retired Naval Officer, Maritime Archaeologist, Anthropology and Archaeology instructor at Clatsop Community College, and founder of the Maritime Archaeological Society. He has an MBA from Troy State University, an MA in

Historical (Maritime) Archaeology from the University of West Florida, and is the author of the fictional maritime adventure *Deep Context*.

Emily Reed: Theodore "Tod" Lundy is an architect with bachelor's degrees in General Science and Architecture from the University of Oregon and a Master of Architecture degree from the University of Pennsylvania. He has taught Architecture at the University of Kansas, Portland State, and King Faisal University of Saudi Arabia. Living in Astoria by the Columbia River and the Pacific Ocean sparked his interest in the history of shipwrecks.

Iowa: Jim Sharpe graduated from Central Washington University with a BS in Anthropology and MS in Resource Management. He has twenty-three years of cultural resources experience in Washington, Oregon, California, Idaho, Nevada, Colorado, and Alaska. Jim has extensive experience with historic agriculture and has authored numerous articles and technical reports on archaeological and historical topics.

Trinidad: Jeff Groth started his working career in commercial diving as a diver tender in the Gulf of Mexico oil fields. He holds a BS in History along with minors in Geography and Anthropology, including an archaeological field school from Portland State University. As a professional cartographer, Jeff has over thirteen years of experience with geographic information systems, GIS, and building archaeological predictive models.

Mauna Ala: Robert Johnson went to the US Merchant Marine Academy and sailed for fifteen years on worldwide bulk carriers. He sailed in all deck officer ranks including master and holds an Unlimited Master's License. Robert recently retired after thirty years as a Columbia River Bar pilot.

INDEX

Townsend, A. G., 132
Trinidad, 119, 136
triple-expansion steam engines,
88, 98, 109
Type TR rescue craft, 112

U
Ullfer, Lew, 91
Underwater Archeological Society
of British Columbia, 61
United States Shipping Board
(USSB), 97, 98
US Army Corps of Engineers,
63, 103

V
Vancouver Island, BC, xi, 29
Vancouver Maritime Museum, 60
Vesey, Captain, 87

W
Washaway Beach, 107, 116, 119
Weaver, J. B., 102
Welch, Capt. John W., 45
West Cadron, 97
Westerlund, Peter, 71

Westport Coast Guard Station,
111, 112, 115
Westport Maritime Museum,
119, 136
Westport South Beach Historical
Society, 107
Wilkes, Lt. Charles, 22, 24
Willapa Bay, xv, 107, 109, 110,
111, 115, 117
Willapa Bay Bar, 109, 110
Willapa Bay Coast Guard Station,
110, 111
Willapa Bay Lighthouse, 110
Willapa River, 109
Williams, Capt. Francis, 41, 42,
43, 45
Williams, Capt. Owen, 84, 85, 87,
88, 90
windjammers, 80, 84, 90
Winslow, Capt. Stewart V., 95
Woods, Roy, 111

Y
Yates, Capt. Edgar L., 96, 99, 103

Z
Zube, Fred, 69, 70, 71, 72

ABOUT THE MARITIME ARCHAEOLOGICAL SOCIETY

The mission of the Maritime Archaeological Society is to seek out, investigate, and document shipwrecks as well as other maritime archaeological sites and to educate the public in areas of maritime cultural heritage, historic shipwreck preservation, and the science of maritime archaeology. The idea for the organization began with several leaders of the Beeswax Wreck Project. With a nonprofit based in Oregon, the team searching for the galleon would be able to apply for state and local grants to help fund the project. Knowing there are thousands of other shipwrecks out there and a shortage of volunteers trained in maritime archaeological survey techniques, an ambitious mission was started to help document shipwrecks and other local submerged archaeological sites in the Pacific Northwest and beyond.

MAS is a citizen science organization working to preserve maritime heritage for everyone. The group is made up of professional archaeologists who donate their time alongside trained volunteers to conduct surveys, both offshore and on land, adding to the public records filed with the State Historic Preservation Office. Volunteers are provided with training in recording maritime heritage and archaeology ethics. MAS does not collect or keep artifacts from wrecks. Artifacts are the property of the public and held in public trust to be displayed.

We work in coordination with state archaeologists and the state park systems. When we record shipwrecks we take only photographs and measurements, leaving the site untouched. It is part of what draws some of us to maritime archaeology. Traditional dirt archaeology is destructive by nature. When significant items do need to be removed for preservation, as was the case with the carronades from *Shark*, state agencies generally take over the task.

While the flagship project remains the Beeswax Wreck, which began nearly ten years prior to the formation of the Maritime Archaeological

Society, the organization has been involved in many other projects. Requests for assistance come from individuals, local historical organizations, governmental organizations, and the National Park Service. Dozens of volunteers have been trained in maritime archaeology techniques, historical research, remote sensing, and remotely operated vehicle (ROV) operations.

Web: maritimearchaeological.org
Instagram: mas_maritime
Facebook: MaritimeArchaeologicalSociety
Twitter: mas_maritime
Contact: info@maritimearchaeological.org